Memory
A Self-Teaching Guide

Carol Turkington

John Wiley & Sons, Inc.

For general information about our other products and services, please contact our
Customer Care Department within the United States at (800) 762-2974, outside the
United States at (317) 572-3993 or fax (317) 572-4002.

Wiley also publishes its books in a variety of electronic formats. Some content that
appears in print may not be available in electronic books.

ISBN: 0-471-39364-9

10 9 8 7 6 5 4 3 2 1

Contents

Introduction

To countless preliterate tribes, memory was the storehouse for the history of their people. To the ancient Greeks and Romans, memory was the key to political success. To more modern memory experts, it was the path to spiritual fulfillment.

But gradually the importance of memory faded, with the advent of the alphabet and the written word. Its value became even less important in the modern age: in our world of typewriters, computers, satellites, and instant communication, memory no longer holds the mystical magic it offered our ancestors. For many in today's world, a good memory is nothing more than a sort of intellectual shorthand, an easier way to study, to succeed in business, to live an organized life.

But in a deeper sense there is far more to memory than recalling dates, finding car keys, or cramming for a history final. It is our memory that transforms a series of unconnected moments into a continuous, unified whole, linking us to our past and pointing the way into the future. We are compassionate because we remember what it is to feel pain. We buttress our lives against disaster because we remember what disaster has cost us in the past. Memory gives us a future more secure than that of creatures who are doomed to repeat their past simply because they cannot remember it. It can rescue us from the fate that awaits those destined to obliteration because they cannot adapt to changed circumstances.

Memory has made possible the development of philosophy and science and song. More personally, it is the repository of our deepest emotions and our most compelling experiences. Memory holds the scent of the sea wind, the sound of a child's laughter, the image of the beloved. It is memory that makes us fully human, because it distills the rich diversity of experience into the essence of the soul.

1 What Is Memory and What Can It Do for You?

Objectives

In this chapter you will learn:

- what memory is
- how memory works
- how to encode a memory
- the key to improving memory

People often talk about memory as if it were a *thing*, like a trick knee or a good head of hair, but in fact your memory doesn't exist in the same way an object exists. Rather, memory refers to the *process* of remembering. Contrary to popular belief, memories aren't plucked fully formed out of little file folders packed away neatly in your brain. Instead, memories represent an incredibly complex constructive power that each one of us possesses.

3

Here's a simple memory test:

1. Remember these words: corn, radio, horse.

2. Remember this name and address: John Brown, 365 Walnut Street, Pittsburgh, Pennsylvania.

3. Name the governor of your state.

4. Name the past two U.S. presidents.

5. What was the main dish you had for breakfast the past two mornings?

6. What were the last two movies you saw in a theater?

7. Have you had more trouble than usual remembering what you've done for the past few weeks?

8. Has it been harder for you to remember names?

9. Have you noticed a decline in your ability to calculate in your head, such as figuring out a tip or correct change?

10. Have you been forgetting to pay bills?

11. Have you had trouble remembering dates?

12. Have you had trouble recognizing people you should know?

13. Have you had a hard time finding the right word you want to use?

14. Have you had trouble remembering how to do simple tasks, such as how to use the stove or a remote control?

15. Do memory problems interfere with your job?

16. Do memory problems interfere with your functioning at home?

17. Does your memory interfere with how well you cope in social situations?

18. What were the three words you were asked to remember at the beginning of the quiz?

19. What was the name and address you were asked to remember at the beginning of the quiz?

Scoring

Questions 3–6	1 point for each answer you were able to give
7–17	1 point for each "no" answer
Bonus points	3 points each for answering 18 and 19 correctly

If you scored . . .

19–21	Great job! You have a better-than-average memory.
16–18	Not bad. You've got an average memory.
11–15	A bit weak. You need to work on the techniques in this book.
0–10	Poor memory. You may need a professional evaluation.

Your baby's first cry . . . the taste of your grandmother's cherry cake . . . the scent of the sea wind. These are memories that are a part of the everyday experiences of your life. Collectively, these memories contribute to making you who you are and help you feel comfortable with familiar people and your surroundings. They serve to connect the past with the present, while providing a structure for the future. This is one of the reasons that the shadow of Alzheimer's disease is so terrifying—if we lose the memories that make us who we are, what do we become?

In the past, many experts have thought of memory as some type of computerlike process lodged somewhere in one section of a person's brain. But today most experts theorize that memory is far more complex and elusive than that. Current researchers believe not that a person's memory is located in one particular place in the brain, but instead that it is a process that takes place *throughout* the brain.

Think about what you had for breakfast this morning. If the image of a big bowl of oatmeal popped into your mind, you didn't concoct that image from some neural pocket in the folds and fissures of your brain. That memory was the result of an incredibly complex process that reassembles different memory impressions from a weblike pattern of cells scattered throughout the brain. Your "memory" is really made up of a group of systems, and each plays a different role in creating, storing, and recalling memories. When the brain processes information normally, all of these different systems work together perfectly so that you are capable of cohesive thought.

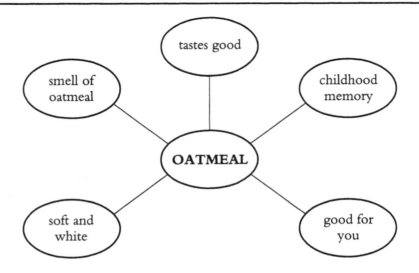

What seems to be a single memory—that bowl of oatmeal—is actually a complex construction. If you think of oatmeal, your brain retrieves its name, its shape, its function, the smell when it's steaming in the bowl—each part of the memory of what "oatmeal" is comes from a different region of the brain. The entire image of "oatmeal" is actively reconstructed by the brain from many different neural areas. Neurologists are only beginning to understand how the parts are reassembled into a coherent whole.

Let's look at another example. If you're riding a horse, the memory of how to ride the horse comes from one set of brain cells, the memory of how to get from here to the end of the paddock comes from another, the memory of horseback-riding safety rules from another, and that nervous feeling you got when your mount slipped going around the corner came from still another. Yet you're never aware of these separate mental experiences, nor of the fact that they're coming from all different parts of your brain, because they work together so well. In fact, experts tell us there is no firm distinction between how you *remember* and how you *think*.

How Does It All Work?

Scientists still don't fully understand exactly *how* we remember or what occurs during recall. The search for the way the brain organizes memories and where those memories are acquired and stored has been a never-ending quest among brain researchers for decades. Still, there is enough information to make some educated guesses.

Encoding a Memory

The process of memory begins with the way information is encoded. Encoding is the first step to creating memory—a biological phenomenon rooted in the senses. For example, if your earliest memory is "mother," your brain probably identified one shape as your mother's blouse, another shape as your mother's face, together with the smell of her clothes, the sound of her voice.

Each of these separate sensations traveled to the part of your brain called the **hippocampus,** which integrates these perceptions as they occur into one single experience: "mother." The hippocampus probably consolidates information for storage as permanent memory in another part of the brain.

Yet while a memory begins with perception, it is encoded and stored in the language of electricity and chemicals. Nerve cells interact with other cells across a tiny gap called a **synapse.** All the action in your brain occurs at these synapses, where electrical pulses carrying messages leap across the gaps between cells. The electrical firing of a pulse across the synapse gap triggers the release of chemical messengers called **neurotransmitters.** These neurotransmitters diffuse across the spaces between cells, attaching themselves to neighboring cells. Each brain cell can form thousands of links like this, giving a typical brain about 100 trillion synapses. The parts of the brain cells that receive these electric impulses are called **dendrites**—feathery tips of brain cells that connect to the neighboring cell.

What is a synapse?

Answer: A synapse is the tiny gap across which a signal is transmitted from one nerve cell to another.

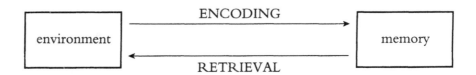

Brain cells function together in a network, organizing themselves into groups that specialize in different kinds of information processing. Yet the connections between brain cells aren't permanent—they can and do change all the time. As one brain cell sends signals to another, the synapse between the two gets stronger. The more active the two brain cells are, the stronger the connection between them grows. This means that with each new experience, your brain slightly rewires its physical structure. In fact, how you use your brain helps determine how your brain is organized. It is this flexibility, which scientists call **plasticity,** that can help your brain rewire itself if it is ever damaged.

As you learn and experience the world, changes occur at the synapses and dendrites, and more connections in your brain are created. In this way, the brain organizes and reorganizes itself in response to your experiences, forming memories triggered by the effects of external input prompted by experience, education, or training.

These changes are reinforced with use, so that as you learn and practice new information, intricate circuits of knowledge and memory are built in the brain. For example, if you play a piece of music over and over, the repeated firing of certain cells in a certain order in your brain make it easier to repeat this firing later on. The result: you get better at playing the music. You can play it faster, with fewer mistakes. Practice it long enough and you will play it perfectly. Yet if you stop practicing for several weeks and then try to play the piece, you may notice that the result is no longer perfect. Your brain has already begun to "forget" what you once knew so well.

To properly encode a memory, you must pay attention. Like most of us, you go through your day ignoring quite a lot of stimuli, so that much of what you encounter every day is simply filtered out. Only a few stimuli pass into your conscious awareness. This is important, because if you remembered every single thing you noticed, your memory would soon become bogged down and overloaded. Therefore, the *way* in which you pay attention to information may be the most important factor in how *much* you remember.

If you want to remember a word, thinking about how it sounds or what it means will help. If you use visual imagery to help you memorize something (for example, meeting a person named Mr. Bell and thinking of a bell when you shake hands), you're more likely to remember it. Some experts believe that using imagery helps you remember because it provides a second kind of memory encoding—and two codes are better than one.

Read the list of words below and try to create a visual picture to go with each word to help you remember it:

stone

smith

barn

rock

tree

bird

young

bean

grin

Memory Stores

Once a memory is created, it must be stored. Many experts think there are three ways we store memories: first comes the sensory stage, when we first notice something. As we perceive something, its registration during perception occurs in the brief "sensory storage" that usually lasts only a fraction of a second. It's our sensory memory that allows a perception such as a visual pattern, a sound, or a touch to linger for a brief moment once the stimulation is over.

After that first flicker, the sensation is stored as short-term memory, a fairly limited cache that lasts for just twenty or thirty seconds before being replaced with other material (unless you constantly repeat it). Most of us find it impossible to remember a phone number after using it the first time, because it's stored only in our ultra-short-term memory. But after using that number more frequently, the information will then become part of our short-term memory; if we use it often enough, ultimately it is stored in long-term memory (also called **retaining**). Unlike sensory and short-term memory, which decay rapidly, long-term memory can store information indefinitely in an unlimited capacity. Most people think of long-term memory when they think of memory itself—but most experts believe that information must first pass through sensory and short-term memory before it can be stored as a long-term memory.

Because there is no need for us to maintain everything in our brain, the different stages of human memory function as a sort of filter that helps to protect us from the flood of information with which we're confronted every day. People tend to store material on subjects they already know something about, since such information has more meaning. This is why someone with a normal memory may be able to remember in depth more information about one particular subject.

Remembering

When you want to remember something, you retrieve the information on an unconscious level, bringing it into your conscious mind at will. While most people think they have either a "bad" or a "good" memory, in fact most of us are fairly good at remembering some things and not so good at others. If you do have trouble remembering something—and assuming you don't have a physical disease—it's usually not the fault of your entire memory system but an inefficient component of one part of your memory system.

Let's look at how you remember where you left your car keys (something many people have trouble with!). If you're going to remember where you left your car keys, you must first register where you placed them. You must be aware of where you are putting them, or you won't remember the location when you need them again. This is where many people go wrong—when they come into the house, they're busy thinking about where they've been or what they're going to tell their spouse now that they're home. They are not paying attention to where they fling their keys.

If you do pay attention to where you've placed the keys, this information will be retained, ready to be retrieved at a later date. If your memory system is working properly, when you go to find your keys you will remember exactly where you left them.

If you've forgotten where they are, one of several things could have happened:

• You may not have registered clearly to start with where you put them down.

- You may not have retained what you registered.

- You may not be able to retrieve the memory accurately.

Therefore, if you want to stop forgetting where you left your keys, you will have to work on improving all three stages of the remembering process. Research suggests that older people in particular have trouble with all three of these stages, but they have special problems with both registering and retrieving information.

If you're forgetting something, it may be that you haven't encoded it very effectively, because you were distracted while the encoding should have taken place. If you've "forgotten" where you put your glasses, you may not have really forgotten at all—instead, the location of your glasses may never have gotten into your memory in the first place. For example, you probably would say that you know what a ten-dollar bill looks like, but most of the time you've not really encoded it, so that if you tried to describe it in detail, you probably couldn't.

Distractions while trying to remember something can interfere with registering your memories. If you're trying to read a complicated tax return in the middle of a busy airport, you may think you're remembering what you read, but you may not be effectively saving it in your memory.

You may forget simply because you're having trouble retrieving the memory. If you've ever tried to remember something one time and couldn't, but then later you remembered that same item, it could be that there was a mismatch between retrieval cues and the encoding of the information you were searching for.

You'll be better able to remember something if you use a "retrieval cue" that occurred when you first formed a memory. If you memorized a poem in your bedroom while Mozart was playing, listening to Mozart again may help you to recall the poem. This is why vivid memories, such as something traumatic, will recur strongly in the presence of an original accompanying sensation—say, why the sound of a car backfiring to a veteran may trigger the unpleasant memories of war.

What's Your Word Span?

One way to test your memory is to take a word-span test. In this exercise have someone read out the following words one set at a time, one word per second. You then repeat the words back.

The first set has just two words in each. The next has three, and so on until you get to seven. You should stop when you can no longer recall all the words in the correct order for all three sets of the same size. The level at which you could recall two of the three sets correctly is your word span.

house	mallet
car	watch
match	bear

cake	grass	hat
meat	poem	cat
bug	lane	bird

pail	sink	hair	dog
game	sea	bean	pillow
banana	cracker	lamp	sock

knife	pencil	radio	year	rabbit
cheese	phone	book	disk	plate
kite	chair	leaf	daughter	wall

bush	cow	gem	slipper	comb	pie
clip	tent	dress	dog	wine	chicken
net	cloud	pot	mouse	dock	fence

stable	driveway	spoon	moose	planet	fence	pin
toes	Indian	game	yard	chip	thief	nurse
heart	globe	rock	smock	beret	number	church

Score: The word span for a typical American college student ranges from 4 to 6.

Summary

In this chapter we discussed the basic process involved in how you re-member: to create a memory, you must first pay attention (notice) it, then retain it, then be able to retrieve it. We don't remember everything; some information is stored only briefly and then fades away; other details enter short-term memory. Only the important information is eventually transferred into long-term memory.

Memories are not stored in one place in the brain but are a process that involves many different parts of the brain all working together. As brain cells work together, the connections between them get stronger. This means that your brain actually changes as you experience the world and as you practice skills over and over again. This is the key to understanding how to improve your memory.

In the next chapter you'll learn that it's possible to improve your memory—but simply sitting down every day and memorizing a page of text won't do it. In fact, what you do *during* that practice is more important than how much time is spent doing it. One study found that three hours of general memory practice did not improve long-term memory, but three hours of practicing using certain techniques did. In this book you'll learn some of these techniques.

SELF-TEST

As a way for you to review what you have read in this chapter, see how many of the questions you can answer without rereading the chapter.

1. Does memory exist in one part of the brain and, if so, where?

2. What is the first stage of creating a memory?

3. To properly encode a memory, what must you do?

4. What are the three ways a memory is stored?

5. If you forget something, the problem may be in one of three components of your memory system. What are these?

ANSWERS

1. Memory does not exist in one part of the brain, but is a constructive process that occurs in many areas.

2. The first stage of creating a memory is encoding or retaining.

3. To properly encode a memory, you must pay attention.

4. Memory is stored in the sensory stage, in short-term memory, and in long-term memory.

5. The components are registering, retention, and retrieval. That is, you may not have registered the information clearly, you may not have retained what you registered, or you may not be able to retrieve the memory accurately.

2

The Keys to a Better Memory

Objectives

In this chapter you will learn:

- what things you have trouble remembering
- the three basic keys to a good memory
- how paying attention pays off
- some effective memory devices

Have you ever walked out of a store and totally forgotten where you left your car? Walked into a room and forgotten what you were doing there? Completely forgotten a crucial word in the middle of a story?

Before you learn the keys to a better memory, it can help to know what sorts of things you have trouble remembering. In the list below please check off each item you tend to forget. If possible, ask family and friends to make sure your answers are accurate. This exercise will help you pinpoint your strengths and weaknesses in different memory areas.

❏ Appointments

❏ Faces

❏ Names

❏ Where you put things

❏ Messages

❏ Deadlines

❏ What you were saying before you were interrupted

❏ Instructions

❏ Directions

❏ Dates

❏ Memory in general

Odds are, when these memory glitches occurred to you at age twenty, you probably didn't give them a second thought. At forty you may begin to fret about having "senior moments" or the approach of menopause. Perhaps you start thinking about using supplements to boost your memory. At sixty many people begin to panic at these same memory glitches and worry whether they might be the first sign of Alzheimer's disease. In fact, most of these "missed memories" are completely normal and have nothing to do with a physical disease.

There are many factors that influence how well a memory is formed, including how familiar the information is and how intently the person is paying attention. Good health also plays a major part in how well a person remembers.

In the previous chapter we learned that scientists don't fully understand *how* a person remembers or what occurs during recall. But what we do know is that it *is* possible to improve your memory. You may think that if you have a bad memory there's nothing you can do about it. In fact, remembering is a learned skill, and it can be developed just like any other skill.

How good your memory is depends on how well you've learned memory skills—it's *not* a function of inborn memory ability. By learning a few simple techniques, it is possible to remember a great deal of information that you once routinely forgot. And while most people assume that memory loss is as inevitable as the aging process, *this is simply not true.*

No matter what kinds of things you have trouble remembering, there are three basic keys that lead to a better memory:

- attention

- association

- visualization

How effectively you work on all three areas can have a direct impact on how well you remember.

Pay Attention!

As generations of students have found out, no matter how thoroughly material is presented, if you're not paying attention, you probably won't remember it. This is also why most people immediately forget someone's name when introduced—they're so busy looking at the new person, making initial judgments, and trying to make pleasant conversation, the name is quickly forgotten.

Paying attention is the most important thing you can do to improve your memory. When you pay attention to something, you decide what elements are worth remembering and which can be ignored or discarded. If something catches your interest, you'll automatically pay attention to it, but if you're bored, you don't have the motivation to concentrate. It's important to understand that paying attention is not a reflex—it's not something you do automatically. You must make a conscious effort to pay attention.

Relax

The first thing you need to do if you want to pay attention is *relax*. It's impossible to pay attention if you're nervous or stressed out. Take a few moments to breathe deeply. Consciously relax the muscles in your shoulders and the back of your neck.

Think Positive

Now tell yourself that you *will* remember. It's important to believe that you'll remember the information, because if you start out by telling yourself it's just too hard to do something, you're going to have trouble remembering it later. If you convince yourself you have a terrible memory no matter what, you're putting yourself at a disadvantage. Remembering is as much attitude as aptitude. It's essential to tell yourself that you can remember *before* you go on to record information.

If you tend to be a daydreamer, this doesn't mean you can't remember well. While it's possible to observe your surroundings absentmindedly, if you really want to remember, you must focus on the information or observation, and concentrate. As you concentrate, really observe. Use all your senses.

Attention Is Fragile

It's also important to understand that paying attention has its limits. Attention is inherently fragile. The average attention span of an audience, for example, is just about twenty minutes. No matter how strong your memory or how powerful your ability to concentrate, after a period of time it's just going to get harder and harder to maintain that focus. This is why all good speakers understand that they need to convey the important parts of their message in the beginning. After a period of about twenty minutes, they know that they must use all sorts of strategies to hold their audience's attention: anecdotes, funny stories, variation in speed and pitch of the voice, and natural pauses.

Don't Divide Attention

Paying attention is crucial to being able to remember—and it's important not to divide your attention. Research suggests that even while you're paying attention to one source, background information you're not paying attention to is still being analyzed. For example, if you've ever been at a party concentrating on one conversation, you will probably notice if a nearby conversational group suddenly mentions your name.

Anyone knows who has ever watched a child eat a snack, do homework, and watch TV at the same time that it is possible to do more than one thing at a time. As long as the tasks don't depend on the same mental processes, it's possible to juggle them all. But if two tasks depend on the same type of mental process—such as reading a book and listening to a story—neither will be accomplished very well. The ability to pay attention to more than one thing at a time varies from person to person and is affected by age, alertness, and motivation. But while it's possible to divide your attention, the best way to remember something is to focus on that one thing while you're learning it. If you're trying to remember someone's name, don't try to listen to a conversation in the next room and a ballgame on TV at the same time.

Anticipate Distractions

In order to fine-tune the ability to pay attention, it's a good idea to anticipate any distractions and eliminate them before they become a problem. If you want your child to do a good job of studying for a test, you should eliminate anything that will interfere with his concentration: TV, radio, music, or other conversations. Switch on the answering machine so calls won't disrupt study time.

1. What is the most important thing you can do to improve your memory?

   _____

2. Why will relaxing help you pay attention?

   _____

3. How long can most people in an audience pay attention?

   _____

   Answers:

   1. Pay attention.

   2. It is impossible to pay attention when you are feeling anxious or stressed.

   3. no more than twenty minutes

Associate

While paying attention is crucial to building a good memory, learning some memory techniques will also help to improve a weak memory. Some of the best techniques involve associating what needs to be remembered with something else.

These techniques are called **mnemonics,** after Mnemosyne, the Greek goddess of memory. Mnemonics (the first *M* is silent) are simple ways to improve or strengthen memory. The most basic mnemonics help you associate something you need to remember with something you already know. If you've ever watched a memory expert amaze an audience with his powers, you're really watching a demonstration of what mnemonics can do.

Hundreds of years ago, before the widespread use of pens and paper or the printing press, these techniques were of profound importance to a society that needed to rely on the power of memory. For the ancient Romans and Greeks, mnemonics were one of the most important subjects taught in classical schools. These memory tricks were used by the greatest orators of the time, who memorized entire speeches this way.

A mnemonic technique isn't a party trick or a way of cheating, but a well-developed method to help you pay attention, register information, and retrieve that information from your memory. The techniques take advantage of the way your brain works in order to boost your ability to recall details. But because they are true *skills,* you need to practice them over and over to become comfortable enough to use them every day. They rely on your innate ability to make associations and organize important information.

For whom are mnemonics named?

Answer: Mnemosyne, the Greek goddess of memory.

Acronyms

One easy way to use an association to help us remember is to use the first letter of a word as a cue to remember the word itself. Acronyms make a word out of the first letters of the words to be remembered. Some acronyms become so familiar we forget that the letters actually stand for something else—the word "scuba," for example, actually stands for "self-contained underwater breathing apparatus." The word "laser" stands for "light amplification by stimulated emission of radiation."

If you want to remember the Great Lakes, you can use the acronym "HOMES" (Huron, Ontario, Michigan, Erie, and Superior). Some acronyms don't necessarily form a real word, as in "NATO" for North Atlantic Treaty Organization.

Acrostics

An acrostic is a related type of first-letter cuing, which turns the first letter of information to be remembered into the first letter of a sentence or poem. For example, if you want to remember the notes on the lines of the treble clef (E, G, B, D, and F) you can remember the sentence: **E**very **G**ood **B**oy **D**oes **F**ine.

To remember the six New England states in descending order (Maine, New Hampshire, Vermont, Massachusetts, Rhode Island, and Connecticut) you could make up this sentence: **M**artha **N**ever **H**ad **V**ery **M**any **R**ed **C**ars.

In the short term, this first-letter cuing can work very well. The primary problem with this method is the tendency to forget the system you came up with in the first place. If you want to avoid this problem, try to make a visual association between the system and what you need to remember. For example, to remember the HOMES acronym, picture a series of large homes floating down the Great Lakes. Spend a lot of time really visualizing these homes so you make a strong impression in your mind. When you try to remember the names of the Great Lakes, the picture of HOMES should come to you, which will then trigger the memory of the acronym you devised.

1. What acronym or acrostic could you come up with to memorize the planets in order of their distance from the sun?

   Mercury

   Venus

   Earth

   Mars

Jupiter

Saturn

Uranus

Neptune

Pluto

_____

_____

2. What acronym or acrostic could you come up with to memorize the strings on a viola (C, G, D, A)?

_____

_____

Popular Sayings

Because they work so well, almost everyone uses a variety of association techniques probably without even realizing it. If you've ever tried to remember whether to turn the clocks back or forward for Daylight Savings Time, you've probably used the saying "Spring forward, fall back" to remember that clocks are turned ahead in May and back in October. And almost every first-grader learns the easy way to keep track of the calendar by reciting the poem "Thirty days hath September . . ."

Poems can be a good way to help remember important information, too, since the rhyme can be an important memory tool. For example, some people who can never remember which way to tighten or loosen a bolt or faucet can remind themselves with this saying: "Lefty loosey, righty tighty."

Visualize

The ability to see a picture in your mind's eye is called visualization, and the more clearly you can see the picture—its shape, color, and form—the better you are at visualizing. Visualizing is really another word for imagining, with great clarity and vividness. It is a skill that some people are better at than others, depending on the way their minds work. It involves the ability to see in pictures, not words—if you think of the word "dog," you *see* an actual dog in your mind, you don't see the word "dog" in letters. Concrete images like "dog" or "cake" are always easier to visualize than are abstract ideas, such as "faithfulness" or "love."

Your imagination can enrich this ability to visualize, so that you can picture the sound, touch, and smell of the object as well. It's possible to visualize the sound and scent of the sea wind, the velvety softness of a deer's nose, or the whiff of morning coffee brewing and bacon frying in the pan.

Visualization is a skill that can improve with practice. Since visualization is extremely important in developing mnemonic skills, it's a good idea to practice visualization skills daily.

Try practicing this visualization exercise each morning as you lie in bed:

1. Close your eyes. Imagine a blueberry pie fresh out of the oven. Feel the warmth of the pie as you carry it from the stove. Sniff the aroma of the hot blueberries.

2. Observe the brown crust and the slits where the steam escaped. Look at the way the blueberry filling has bubbled through the crust, hardening along the pie pan.

3. Place the pie on the counter and pick up a knife. Feel the heft of the knife's handle as you slice into the pie.

4. Remove a slice and place it on a plate. Watch the blueberries ooze out the sides from beneath the crust.

5. Take a fork and slide it into the dough. Put the fork into your mouth and taste the blueberries. Taste the liquid filling and the warm, flaky pastry. If there's ice cream on the pie, taste the contrast between the cold ice cream and the heat of the berries.

If you're a good observer, you're probably good at visualizing as well. People who don't spend much time paying attention to their surroundings are going to have a harder time bringing them into focus in their mind's eye. The better you are able to pay attention to what's around you, the better you will be able to visualize later.

Here's a good exercise to see how well you've been paying attention to your living space:

1. Write an accurate description of your wristwatch. Describe it in complete detail. Draw an accurate picture of the watch.

   _____

   _____

   _____

2. Write an accurate description of your desk and all the items on it. Describe each item: stapler, pens, clock, blotter, and so on.

   _____

   _____

   _____

3. Describe a favorite picture and its frame hanging on a wall in your home. Include as many details as you can.

   _____

   _____

   _____

Practice!

The most important key to a better memory is daily practice. If you want to learn to drive a car, you don't just study the owner's manual and then jump behind the wheel and drive through New York City. You may understand the mechanics, but putting what you've learned into practice takes repetition. In the same way, you need to keep practicing the memory techniques you will learn in this book.

Actively search for things to memorize, such as your friend's phone number, your neighbor's license plate, the vocabulary words in your French textbook, your driver's-license number, or all your credit-card numbers. If you run into trouble, don't give up. Keep practicing, and you'll succeed.

Make It Real

Practice visualization each day. Pick items from the following list and make it as vivid and real in your mind as you can.

birch tree

pool

new kitten

overcoat

camera

doctor's appointment

first date

warm oatmeal cookies

campfire

mountaintop cabin

Summary

In this chapter we discussed how it's possible to improve your memory by practicing a set of skills each day. There are three keys to a better memory:

- attention

- association

- visualization

When you're paying attention, remember to relax, think positively, anticipate distractions, and realize that there is a limit to how long you can focus your concentration.

While paying attention is crucial, you must also learn memory techniques that involve associating what needs to be remembered with something else. Acronyms are a way to remember words by using the first letter of each word to make another word as a cue to remember the word itself. An acrostic is a related type of first-letter cuing, which turns the first letter of information to be remembered into the first letter of a word, sentence, or poem. Popular sayings are yet a third way to associate something to be remembered with something else, such as "Thirty days hath September." Finally, visualizing is a good way to associate something that needs to be remembered with something else that you will recall easily.

SELF-TEST

To review what you've read, see how many of these questions you can answer without rereading the chapter.

1. What factors go into how well a memory has formed?

2. Is memory loss inevitable as you age?

3. What are the three basic keys to a good memory?

4. What is a person's average attention span?

ANSWERS

1. how familiar the information is, how much the person is paying attention, and how healthy the person is

2. While most people assume that memory loss is inevitable as we age, *this is simply not true.*

3. attention, association, and visualization

4. twenty minutes

3   Improving Everyday Memory

In this chapter you will learn:

- helpful mental exercises to boost brain power
- how lifestyle changes can help memory
- three things to help diminish general forgetfulness

Do you forget where you parked your car? Can you remember when you have a haircut appointment? Do you constantly misplace your glasses? If you're healthy but having problems with your memory, it's possible to halt the downward trend and reverse a recalcitrant short-term memory. One of the best ways to keep your memory sharp—or to improve it if it's starting to fail—is to practice a lot of mental exercises. Of course, your brain isn't a muscle that needs to be physically strengthened. Instead, what the brain does best is communicate with its own cells, and the faster it can communicate—with healthier and more numerous connections between cells—the better your mind will work, and the more your memory will improve.

You can keep your brain nimble by doing puzzles, riddles, and other brain-challenging exercises, which strengthens the connections between cells and builds new connections. Research has found that the more connections there are, the faster your mind can work. Any activity that engages the brain, such as chess, riddles, or puzzles (even watching TV, if it's a program that actively engages you), can help. Stimulating the senses, facing new physical challenges, learning to play an instrument or speak a foreign language—all help build more cellular bridges within the brain and can improve overall brain function.

Mental Exercises

One of the most popular methods for getting those brain cells working is to solve puzzles or riddles, which force you to think in unusual or creative ways. Puzzles and riddles help exercise your mind because they involve mathematics, logical reasoning, patterns, and nonlinear thinking.

Serial Subtraction

Try problems such as this one to exercise your brain and improve your memory:

1. Think of a three-digit number, say, 826.
2. Mentally subtract 6.
3. Now mentally subtract 6 from that.
4. Keep subtracting 6 until there's nothing more to subtract.

You can try this with any number you choose. The key is to practice and do the calculations mentally—no calculators or pencils.

Brain Exercise

Try the following riddle to exercise the brain cells:

If you have a five-gallon jug and a three-gallon container, how would you measure one gallon of water using only these two items?

Answer: First fill the three-gallon container with water. Pour it all into the five-gallon jug. Fill up the three-gallon container again and pour the water into the five-gallon jug until it's full. You will now have one gallon of water left in the three-gallon container.

Verb-Noun Activity

Think of a noun: for example, DOG. Now add a verb. The DOG DUG. The DOG JUMPED. The DOG BARKED. Keep going until you've exhausted your verb repertoire. Now add an adjective to each noun-verb combo: The BLACK DOG DUG. The FRIGHTENED DOG JUMPED. The ANGRY DOG BARKED. Now add an adverb. The BLACK DOG DUG FURIOUSLY. The FRIGHTENED DOG JUMPED HIGH. The ANGRY DOG BARKED LOUDLY.

Enrich Your Life

While puzzles and games are obvious choices for keeping memory sharp, it also helps to expose yourself to new and interesting environments. Research with animals has clearly shown that unusual and stimulating environments can stop the brain from shrinking with age and can actually improve brain-cell connections and boost memory skills. Rats who lived in cages with plenty of exciting toys and lots of stimulation had larger, healthier brain cells and larger outer-brain layers. Deprived rats living in barren cages with no toys had smaller brains.

So don't be a couch potato! Get out and see new places, do new things. Take up a sport or start a hobby. Visit museums or places of interest in your town you've never taken the time to investigate before. Learn a foreign language. Take up chess. Stretch!

If you stay active, interested in life, and engaged in the world, your memory doesn't have to deteriorate as you age. Make sure your home environment is stimulating and enriched, with lots of colors, sounds, smells, and things to do. Anything that engages the senses will also improve your mind and strengthen your memory—so touch, feel, smell, and experience new things.

Here are some ideas to get you started:

- Make sure you have music playing every day. Any music is good, but research suggests that classical music is especially stimulating to the intellect.

- Add lots of books to the room—and read them, don't just look at them.

- Try some challenging books. "Beach reads" are okay for fun, but choose a more difficult book sometimes that makes you stop and think about what you're reading.

- Add a fish tank with lots of colorful fish and interesting tank toys.

- Paint the walls interesting, unusual colors, or add some wallpaper. Select interesting art, rugs, and curtains. Use lots of different textures.

- If you have the space, put out a few birdhouses and feeders by a window and keep a pair of binoculars handy. Plant some brightly colored flowers outdoors, and hang a hummingbird feeder.

- Don't forget the flowers indoors, too—the colors and smells will be an added sensory boost.

- Set out a jigsaw puzzle or chessboard and regularly engage visitors in a game.

- Plug in a computer and use it to surf the Internet or play a challenging game. Computer games can improve memory in such fun ways you'll hardly notice the effort.

- Eat ethnic food you've never before sampled.

- Choose one new recipe a week to try out on your family.

Visualization

Visualization is one of the biggest keys to memory tricks we'll discuss later in the book. But it's also good at boosting brain power by making your brain work in new and unusual ways. Visualization helps stimulate the mind and can also be a great relaxation tool at the same time.

As you sit in your car in a traffic jam, wait for a doctor's appointment, or lie in bed before you fall asleep, practice visualizing something from your childhood:

- the interior of the house where you grew up

- your first-grade classroom

- your childhood best friend's bedroom

- the inside of the car your parents owned when you were a teenager

Lifestyle Changes

You've probably noticed that some days you wake up feeling perky and your memory seems sharp as a tack. Other days, when you're under stress or feeling sick, depressed, or anxious, your mind feels completely foggy. You might be preoccupied, or perhaps you're dwelling on negative feelings. This is the time when you're going to have the most problems with your memory.

The importance of the link between mind and body is becoming more accepted in mainstream medicine as scientists discover more about the connection between the way we feel and how our body works. Your memory is a part of how your brain functions, so it follows that anything that interferes with brain function is going to interfere with how you store and retrieve information. You know that how well you pay attention affects how well you remember, so any outside distraction or emotional problem that interferes with attention is going to interfere with how well you remember. This is why your memory is affected by diet, smoking, caffeine, alcohol, exercise, sleep, stress levels, anxiety, relaxation, depression, and medications.

Diet

If it's true that you are what you eat, it's also true that what you eat directly affects how well you can remember. Indeed, some studies suggest that there is a link between certain foods and memory. Deficiencies of almost any nutrient can impair nervous system function, and imbalances in certain vitamins and minerals appear to play a part in memory problems. Water is also important in maintaining memory systems, especially in the elderly. Dehydration has a direct and profound effect on memory, causing confusion and thinking problems.

Essential nutrients like proteins, carbohydrates, fats, lecithin, and the B vitamins are important for enhancing mental processes such as registering, retaining, and remembering. Some of the strongest research studies have found that eating the right type of fat—monounsaturated fat—can protect memory, perhaps by helping to maintain the structure of the brain cell membrane.

Until researchers really understand the complex ways that nutrition affects memory, the best idea is to eat a balanced diet of a variety of

Diet Plan

How is your diet? Write down a day's worth of the food you consumed, and indicate how what you ate affected your memory and mood.

Morning _____
_____
_____

Noon _____
_____
_____

Night _____
_____
_____

Bedtime _____
_____
_____

Snacks _____
_____
_____

dairy products; breads and cereals; vegetables and fruits; seafood, poultry, and meats; together with enough thiamine, folate, and B$_{12}$. It's also a good idea to avoid eating large amounts of food right before starting a thinking task, since this diverts blood to the stomach, impairing mental performance and distracting the mind during the critical registration and remembering phases. For this reason you should eat only a light meal before giving a speech, taking a test, or attending class.

Smoking

While you may have the impression that smoking is sharpening your mind, in fact studies have shown that puffing on a regular nicotine cigarette can impair memory as much as several alcoholic drinks can. Non-smokers are able to remember lists of numbers more quickly than are

---

How Much Do You Smoke?

How do your cigarettes affect your memory? Write down each cigarette you smoked today, and indicate how it affected your feelings, thoughts, and memory.

Morning _____

_____

_____

Noon _____

_____

_____

Night _____

_____

_____

Bedtime _____

_____

_____

smokers, and they also score higher on standard memory tests. While smoking may enhance performance of simple tasks, it interferes with more complex cognitive processes (including memory).

In addition, research indicates that smokers who want to remember something should put off lighting up right before a memory task (but putting off smoking too long beforehand can make a smoker so jittery that it distracts from the task). Scientists think smoking interferes with memory by slowing down the blood supply carrying oxygen to the brain.

Caffeine

While the caffeine in a cup of coffee or tea amounts to a mild stimulant and may keep you awake enough to pay attention, it also can make you too jittery to learn and remember. In fact, caffeine is just as likely to have a negative effect on memory as a positive one. Studies have shown that a person who is already wide awake and rested won't get much of a memory boost from caffeine, but too much coffee (and the exact amount varies from person to person) can bring on jitters, insomnia, and memory problems. For a habitual user, not getting the accustomed dose of caffeine can have the same negative effect.

Caffeine acts on the brain, affecting coordination, concentration, sleep patterns, and behavior. The gastrointestinal tract absorbs most of the caffeine and distributes it to all tissues and organs within minutes of consumption; maximum blood levels are reached within forty-five minutes. While caffeine thus may improve simple motor tasks, it may disrupt more complex tasks involving fine motor coordination and quick reactions. Of course, any drug's effect depends on the amount consumed and how often, on how much the body absorbs, and how quickly it's metabolized.

However, not to worry if you enjoy an occasional cup. Research does suggest that very small amounts of caffeine probably do no permanent memory harm, which is comforting, since it's found in a wide variety of products. In addition to food and beverages, caffeine crops up in over-the-counter stimulants, painkillers, cold preparations, antihistamines, and prescription drugs. In fact, more than two thousand nonprescription drugs and more than a thousand prescription medications contain caffeine or caffeine-type stimulants.

Caffeine

How does caffeine affect your memory? Write down each cup of coffee or tea or each cola drink you had today, and indicate how it affected your memory and behavior.

Morning _____

_____

_____

Noon_____

_____

_____

Night_____

_____

_____

Bedtime_____

_____

_____

Alcohol

Alcoholic beverages interfere with the capacity to learn and slow down mental functions that can lead to defective recording and storage of memory. Alcohol abuse can lead to even more serious memory problems; even a few drinks four times a week can lower your ability to remember.

Indeed, short-term memory loss is a classic problem among people who abuse alcohol. The potential for difficulty is based not on the number of ounces drunk per day but on each person's individual tolerance for alcohol. Some people over age forty experience the most memory problems after drinking, but even people aged twenty-one to thirty can experience memory loss following excessive alcohol abuse.

Alcohol

How does alcohol affect your memory? Write down each drink you had today (or on a recent day), and indicate how it affected your memory and behavior.

Morning _____

_____

_____

Noon _____

_____

_____

Night _____

_____

_____

Bedtime _____

_____

_____

In addition, women appear to be more vulnerable to the toxic effects of alcohol, especially in relation to short-term memory. Among alcoholics, women seem to suffer from both verbal and spatial thinking problems, whereas men seem to be affected only by spatial cognitive difficulties.

Most alcohol-related memory problems seem to fade away when the person stops drinking, although a lifetime of abuse may cause irreversible damage.

Exercise

If you want to boost your memory, it's a good idea to get up off that couch and start exercising. Studies suggest that aerobic exercise can help maintain short-term memory, especially as it applies to general-memory and verbal-memory tests. This type of memory is particularly important in recalling names, directions, and telephone numbers or in pairing a name with a face. Experts believe that exercise may help improve memory by increasing oxygen efficiency to the brain or boosting metabolism.

1. How much exercise do you get per week? List all activities ranging from sports to work around the house and the amount of time spent on each one.

_____
_____
_____
_____

2. If you spent less than thirty minutes three times per week on exercise, devise an action plan to improve this amount.

_____
_____
_____
_____

Sleep

If you've got a business presentation in the morning or a big test the next day you're liable to stay up and cram the night before—which is actually the worst way to prepare for a memory task.

While you're sleeping, your brain's job is to revise and store memories. During certain periods of deep sleep (about every hour and a half), your brain disconnects from the senses and processes, reviews, consolidates, and stores memory. If you interrupt this critical period, it will seriously affect your subsequent performance. Staying up most of the night therefore deprives you of the valuable memory-consolidation period during rest, and it also interferes with learning during waking hours.

When you wake up after a good night's sleep, you feel refreshed and alert, so you are well prepared for memory tasks. For this reason you should avoid sleeping pills, which usually do not provide refreshing sleep and can make you even less alert when you wake up.

Stress and Anxiety

If you've been under a lot of stress, don't be surprised if you have problems with your memory. Prolonged exposure to high levels of cortisol (the hormone produced in the body in response to high stress) has a negative effect on memory, although it takes several days of stress from major surgery or severe psychological trauma in order for cortisol to produce memory impairment.

Memory problems can appear after everything from severe short-term stress to less severe but long-term chronic stress. However, evidence suggests that these kinds of cortisol levels are not harmful to the brain. While it is possible that sustained, high levels of stress can make brain cells vulnerable to other types of injury, scientists don't believe that the memory impairments related to stress are irreversible.

Generalized anxiety often appears hand in hand with stress, and it can be a major cause of memory problems. When anxiety becomes pronounced, it can monopolize your attention to the point where you find it impossible to concentrate on anything else. Because the formation of memory depends on paying attention, anything that interferes with attention will interfere with memory, too.

Anxiety attacks can also affect memory. These attacks involve a pervasive feeling of anxiety not associated with anything in particular. In the midst of an anxiety attack, the sufferer withdraws from the exterior world and turns inward, focusing on internal turmoil. This is why the person fails to record information the way he or she normally would. When the thought processes are occupied exclusively with negative thoughts, there is no room for other thoughts that would cue memory.

There are a number of good ways to ease everyday stress:

- Self-talk: Tell yourself, "I am going to calm down now and pay strict attention if I want to remember this."

- Breathing: Practice breathing in and out slowly and deeply. Breathe from the diaphragm—push your stomach out as you breathe in.

- Self-hypnosis: Close your eyes, count to ten, and imagine yourself floating gently downward on a cloud.

- Visualization: Imagine yourself in the middle of a relaxing scene; imagine taking your worries and dropping them into a trash can.

Depression

It is quite clear that depression and memory problems coincide. In fact, doctors consider memory and concentration problems to be warning signs of depression. Depression alters brain chemistry in a way that lowers the level of attention and reduces the capacity to concentrate, both factors that can interfere with memory.

Depressed people may have problems remembering recent and sometimes even past events. Other memory processes most affected by depression include the recall of positive words (incongruent with the person's depressed mood), immediate recall, and recognitition of verbal stimuli.

One day a depressed person's memory may work well, and the next day she finds she can't remember anything. Depressed people can't concentrate, and they often feel confused and bewildered. Some depressed people may ramble, finding it hard to keep to one conversational topic.

Studies have shown that many depressed people aren't very good at storing information that requires focused attention. In one study testing the memory of thirty-two depressed people, the depressed patients tended to use more passive approaches to remembering. The more depressed a person is, the more likely that the person will also have trouble remembering.

In some cases depression can closely mimic dementia, especially among older people. It's such a problem that many older people in nursing homes who seem overly forgetful and even demented are simply assumed to be senile and are not correctly diagnosed and treated for depression. In fact, one report indicates that depression is so common among those over age sixty-five that 13 percent need antidepressant medication.

Depression, whether present alone or in combination with dementia, can be reversed with proper treatment, which usually involves a combination of medication and cognitive therapy. The difference between dementia and depression is important to recognize: A depressed person will anguish over forgetfulness, whereas a demented person will try to hide memory problems. A depressed person makes little effort to perform tasks, whereas a demented person will struggle to perform well.

Medications

Today's medications may seem like miracle drugs, but a surprising number of them can interfere with memory. Combinations of drugs are even more likely to cause problems in mental sharpness.

Chemotherapy

Chemotherapy drugs are among the newest group of medications that have been found to damage memory. According to some initial research, ordinary levels of chemotherapy seem to dull patients' intellectual powers permanently, leaving them with poor memory recall and muddy thinking.

Patients who are given standard chemotherapy appear to be about twice as likely as other cancer patients to score poorly on various intelligence tests an average of ten years after their treatment, according to a Dartmouth Medical School study. As a result, some doctors believe the findings suggest that aggressive treatment with chemotherapy may be unwise in some people with early-stage cancer unless the drugs are likely to substantially improve chances of survival.

Many years after treatment some cancer survivors say they still have trouble remembering and concentrating. Some say they need a calculator for math problems they once could have solved in their heads. Others have to read a page twice to absorb what's being said.

During treatment many people feel unfocused because they are anemic, sick from the chemotherapy, and sleepy from antinausea medicines, but intellectual ability gradually returns as they recover. For some patients, however, intellect does not return to pretreatment levels. In one study, between a quarter and a third of those who got chemotherapy scored near the bottom in at least four of nine areas of intellectual ability that researchers measured. Only half as many of the patients who underwent surgery or radiation alone did this badly. Earlier studies have found a chance of lingering intellectual impairment in people who receive high-dose chemotherapy, such as those undergoing bone-marrow transplants.

Psychoactive Drugs

Any medication that causes drowsiness is capable of affecting memory, including:

- benzodiazepines (including Valium and Ativan)
- neuroleptics
- some antidepressants
- lithium

While many of these drugs do impair memory, different drug classes may not cause the same type of memory deficit. In fact, drugs in the same class don't all cause the same type or amount of memory loss. For example, one type of antidepressant that interferes with serotonin reuptake may improve memory, compared to the tricyclic antidepressants that interfere with memory.

Anticholinergic Drugs

These drugs block acetylcholine and are used to treat irritable bowel syndrome and certain types of urinary incontinence, Parkinson's disease, asthma, and other diseases. They also have a reputation as amnesiac drugs. Blocking acetylcholine prevents the communication between nerve cells, which alters behavior. Depending on the dose, scopolamine, atropine, and glycopyrrolate all produce sedation and lack of vigilance, which can cloud memory. Scopolamine, a belladonna alkaloid, is a particularly potent memory blocker. Other anticholinergics include some antidepressants, antipsychotics, antihistamines, anti-Parkinson's drugs, and some hypnotics.

Research suggests that after a person receives an anticholinergic drug, it becomes harder for that person to retrieve memories. Scientists suspect that the neurochemical processes disrupted by these drugs aren't involved in maintaining information in memory, but control the encoding process which leads to a problem in retrieving memory.

Neurological Drugs

Neurological drugs (drugs used for brain problems) have been less extensively studied. All the older antiepileptic drugs are considered harmful to memory, as are atropine derivatives, which typically induce amnesia. In particular, phenytoin (Dilantin) is an antiepileptic drug that in large doses can impair memory, reaction time, and intelligence.

Other Drugs

Many other medications also may cause memory problems, including quinidine, naproxen, opiates, some antibiotics, antihistamines, and interferons. Other drugs that can affect memory include drugs to treat high blood pressure, painkillers, insulin, beta blockers (especially those used to control glaucoma), methyldopa, seasickness patches, and certain antiepileptic drugs.

Inhalants

Inhaling fumes of common household products, such as paint thinner, spray paint, mimeograph fluid, or hairspray, can lead to memory problems and learning disabilities. Inhalants can damage the brain, killing brain cells by dissolving the protective myelin sheath that surrounds the nerves. In the cerebral cortex many inhalants cause permanent brain damage, memory problems, learning disabilities, personality changes, hallucinations, and death. By affecting cells in the cerebellum (the brain center for balance and coordination), many inhalants also can cause temporary or permanent loss of coordination, slurred speech, tremors, and Parkinson's-like symptoms.

What kinds of drugs can impair memory?

Answer: Chemotherapy drugs, benzodiazepines, neuroleptics, antidepressants, lithium, anticholinergic drugs, neurological drugs such as phenytoin; quinidine, naproxen, opiates, antibiotics, antihistamines, interferons, drugs to treat high blood pressure, painkillers, insulin, beta blockers, methyldopa, seasickness patches, certain antiepileptic drugs, and inhalants.

Head Injury

If you want to keep your memory sharp, it's a good idea to protect your skull. New research links trauma not only to memory loss but also to the later development of Alzheimer's disease. Even the mildest bump on the head might damage your brain to some extent; in fact, research suggests that 60 percent of people who experience a mild brain injury are still having trouble with memory as long as three months later.

Mild head injury symptoms can result in a puzzling interplay of behavioral, cognitive, and emotional complaints that make the problems difficult to diagnose. Symptoms after a head injury may be caused by direct physical damage to the brain, as well as by swelling or a lack of oxygen.

The type of accident determines the kind of injury the brain receives. In a closed head injury, if the head was restrained on impact, the maximum damage will be found at the impact site; a moving head will result in a "contrecoup" injury, in which damage will occur on the side opposite the point of impact. Both kinds of injuries cause swirling movements throughout the brain, tearing nerve fibers and resulting in widespread blood vessel damage. There may be bleeding in the brain that leads to a bruise or swelling, which can block oxygen to the brain.

Both direct and diffuse effects may cause memory deficits after a head injury. In most cases, however, permanent, severe memory loss with intact functioning in other areas doesn't occur.

After a head injury there may be problems with confusion, disorientation, amnesia, and difficulty storing and retrieving new information. For some reason the physical and emotional shock of the accident interrupts the transfer of all information that happened to be in the short-term memory just before the accident; that's why some people can remember information from several days before and after an accident but not information from immediately before the accident. The length of the unconscious period is linked to how well the person recovers after the head injury. Temporary amnesia after head injury often starts with a loss of memory for things that happened weeks, months, or years before the injury, but this will improve over time.

In particular, football injuries—which may involve repeated trauma to the skull—can lead to later neurological problems. In one study more than half of the retired players surveyed had experienced concussions, and as a group these players were more likely to have memory problems. Many neurologists are convinced that concussions, as well as repeated blows to the head, do lasting damage to the memory processes. The most commonly cited anecdotal example is the "punch-drunk" syndrome of speech and movement impairments and other abnormalities seen in some retired boxers. But people who sustain head injuries from many other causes also experience memory difficulties. In fact, memory disorders are among the top three complaints of patients with traumatic brain injury.

Mnemonic Strategies

In addition to lifestyle changes, there are some memory strategies you can start right now to improve your memory. Not all aspects of memory slow down as you age, so it's important to know that you can compensate for most problems by using memory tricks.

General Forgetfulness

If you're plagued with general everyday forgetting, it could mean that your life is simply a bit out of control. Excess stress, lots of responsibilities, and plenty of distractions may be interfering with your ability to pay attention—which then interferes with your ability to remember.

You are most likely to be absentminded when you're preoccupied or if you're in the middle of a regular routine or familiar environment. Absentminded daydreamers or those who are easily distracted are especially vulnerable to interference. Here's a quick list of ways to improve this very common type of general forgetfulness:

1. **Get organized:** Develop a routine and stick to it. If you're organized, you can often make up for not remembering certain things by keeping information and various possessions in easily accessible places.

2. **Be neat:** Always have a place for everything, and put everything in its place. If you have a key rack right inside your door, you'll be more likely to hang your keys there and remember where they are. A basket by the bedside for glasses means you'll always know where they are when you're not wearing them.

3. **Keep duplicates:** If you can never find your reading glasses when you want them, consider multiple pairs. (You can buy inexpensive reading glasses in discount stores.) Keep one pair in your car, one in your purse, one by the bed. The same goes for scissors or pens—they're not expensive, and it frees you from trying to remember where you left them if you've got spares in every room.

4. **Make a to-do list:** Keep a daily to-do list and cross off items once they've been done. Always keep the list in one place, and organize it into categories. Make your list easy to find—use large, colored sheets of paper. The kitchen is a good spot to post it.

5. **Use a calendar:** Have a calendar handy to keep track of important dates. Check the calendar the same time every day, so it becomes a habit. When you buy a new calendar at the beginning of the year, transfer all important dates from the old one.

6. **Prepare:** If you need to remember to take certain things to work or school, keep a tote bag or backpack right by the front door. Transfer all papers and items that need to go with you into that bag or backpack.

7. **Focus:** Focus on one thing at a time, and try to pay active attention each time you put something down.

8. **Make visual cues:** Place a colored sticky note on your steering wheel or protruding from your briefcase or purse, stick one on your office chair or your bathroom mirror, your shoes or your wallet. Don't assume you'll remember; leave plenty of reminders.

9. **Keep important numbers in one place:** This is a guarantee that you can locate them even if you're under a lot of stress. Be sure to keep these numbers in your wallet:
   - Phone numbers for doctors, emergency contact, neighbors
   - Medical insurance and social security numbers
   - License plate and car insurance numbers

10. **Replace:** Return frequently used things to the same place each time, and rely on placement to trigger your memory (for example, leave an umbrella on a doorknob).

11. **Associate:** Make associations between an item like a badminton set and its use, say at a birthday party.

12. **Repeat:** If someone tells you information that you need to remember, repeat it over and over again.

13. **Think positively:** Keep a positive attitude about memory lapses. Be sensitive to the many things that can make you prone to forget. You can take action to overcome or mitigate most of them.

If you want to focus on minimizing your everyday forgetting, it helps to pinpoint where the problem is. In the past week, did you do any of the following?

____ left iron on

____ forgot to turn off stove

____ forgot to turn off other appliance

____ left door unlocked

____ forgot to feed pets

____ left TV on

____ left radio playing

____ misplaced keys

____ misplaced glasses

____ misplaced credit card

____ misplaced checkbook

____ misplaced cell phone

____ misplaced cordless phone

____ misplaced TV remote

____ forgot appointment

____ forgot birthday or anniversary

Some people excel at remembering names, while others are good at remembering small details. It's unrealistic to expect to remember everything—but with some practice you can get better at remembering those things you're not so good at remembering.

"Everyday forgetting" is linked to the fact that you've run through your daily routines so many times in the past, it can be hard to remember if on *this particular day* you've turned off the stove or unplugged the iron. Some people go through entire routines of "checking" in the morning because they know they have problems remembering whether they've actually turned off appliances before leaving for the day.

Paying Attention

If you really want to cure your memory problem, you need to become acutely aware of what you're doing. When you don't pay attention, you're not likely to register information in the first place. The likely result: forgetting.

Paying attention takes effort. There may be times when your attention strays. Think of the times you rush out the door, forgetting something. Instead, you need to slow down and pause. It is important to pay attention to and concentrate on what you are doing.

For example, have you ever suddenly become unsure as you are driving to work about whether or not you unplugged the iron before you left the house? To improve your ability to remember these everyday events, you need to pause and pay attention as you turn off or unplug an appliance so that it will register in your memory. This helps to make an automatic act conscious.

Here are the steps:

1. Stop. Before going out the door, say, "Where am I going? What do I need to do?"

2. Breathe deeply. Slow down and take the time to think. Focus your concentration.

3. Speak out loud to force yourself to pay attention. If you often forget to turn off the stove, go into the kitchen and make yourself slowly survey the appliances. As you look at each one, say, "The oven is turned off. The toaster is turned off." *Say this out loud.* When you're driving down the freeway and you start to ask yourself if the oven is off, you'll know that it is, because saying so out loud reinforced the memory.

4. If you tend to leave important things behind, line them all up by the door before you leave. Go through each item, naming it out loud. Check your calendar to assure yourself that everything you need is lined up and ready.

5. Take immediate action. Do you need to return that library book or video? Do it *now*—while you're thinking about it. If you can't do it at the moment you think of it, at least put the book or video by the front door. Lean it right up against the door if you have to.

The more harried you are, the harder it can be to remember the everyday details of your life. You need a system, which is why people rely on calendars, electronic organizers, day-timers, computerized reminders, and other memory aids. Here are some strategies to handle specific memory problems:

Remembering Habitual Tasks

If you have trouble remembering habitual tasks such as brushing your teeth each morning or feeding the cat, the key to solving this problem is to relate the activity to something you *won't* forget to do every day. For example, if you forget to use your deodorant in the morning, tell yourself each day that you won't eat breakfast until you find your roll-on. By incorporating a task into an outline of things you don't forget to do, you're less likely to forget that task.

Organization is the key. The more organized and routine your life, the lower the risk you have of forgetting anything. This is why older people actually have less of a problem with absentmindedness than younger folks do; their lives rely far more on a daily routine.

Recalling Where You Put Things

There is hope for those who can't remember where they left their car keys or their purse. As discussed above, the main reason people forget is that they weren't paying attention when they dropped their keys on the hall table, the nightstand, or the kitchen counter. Because they weren't paying attention in the first place, when it comes time to retrieve the memory of where they left the object—they can't. They never properly stashed it in short-term memory to begin with.

This problem is compounded by the fact that they have probably dropped keys or glasses in many different places many different times, so when they *do* recall leaving them somewhere, they may not be recalling the most recent place.

As we read above, the first rule is really quite simple: *Pay attention*. All you have to do is pay attention to where you are placing the keys. Stop yourself in the middle of dropping them on the desk and take a deep breath. Stare at the desk and say out loud: "I am putting my keys on the desk." If you force yourself to pay attention, you won't forget when it comes time to retrieving that particular memory. You may feel foolish, but it's a sure bet you'll remember where you left your keys.

If you can't pay attention, at least *be consistent!* Be sure to put the object back in exactly the same place every single time. Find specific places to keep all the items that are often misplaced:

- glasses

- keys

- medications

- coupons

- TV remote

- cell phone

- cordless phone

TV Remote and Phone Tips

Consider attaching a "homing device" on your TV remote that beeps when you clap your hands. Cordless phones are a real boon to our busy modern lives—but not if the last person to use the phone simply left it on the sofa instead of back on the base unit. If you find yourself losing track of the cordless phone, it can often be located by pressing the "intercom" button on the base unit; the handset will then beep, and you can track it down.

Remembering Where You Parked

It's not unusual to forget where you've parked the car in a large parking lot. Here's how to remember:

1. After you park your car, don't just get out of the car and head straight for your destination. Stop.

2. Look around and make a mental note of where you are. Find something that will help you remember. Did you park next to a tall lamppost? Is there a reference number or letter posted to help you find your way?

3. Better yet, write a description of the location on the garage ticket or another slip of paper and put it somewhere easy to find.

4. Don't rely on a description of the cars around you—they could very well be gone when you come back to your car.

5. If all else fails, try making your car stand out. Tie a red ribbon or a brightly patterned flag to the antenna. This way you'll be sure to find your way!

Remembering Your Schedule

Knowing that you need to do something in the future won't matter if you then forget to do it at the right time. For example, a week before the tax deadline you may remember that you need to mail in your IRS payment, but if you forget all about the task on the day you intended to do it and the deadline passes, you haven't solved your problem. In fact, a problem with remembering dates is one of the most common memory failures there is. A combination of mental strategies and mechanical reminders should help get this under control.

One way to solve the problem of forgetting a date is to cue your attention. For example, you could take your IRS payment and tape it to the front door or, if that makes you too nervous, tape a dollar bill to the front door to remind yourself. Here are some other memory cues:

- Attach a safety pin to your sleeve.

- Put a rubber band around your wrist.

- Move your watch to the opposite arm.

- Leave a note to yourself (brightly colored Post-its are ideal) in a prominent place.

Using a calendar is an excellent mechanical method of remembering dates. The key is not to use *two* calendars—one at home and one at work. If you do, you're asking for trouble when you forget to transfer an important date and schedule two things for the same day.

Instead, get *one* calendar either small enough to carry with you or large enough to tack up at home so everyone can see it. Some people swear by computer calendars that they can access both at home and at work.

Whatever calendar you ultimately choose, all important days should be marked down. Consult the calendar every morning and cross off items as they occur. On the first day of the new year, get out a new calendar and transfer all the important dates from the old calendar so you don't forget anything.

Remembering What You're Doing

Have you ever gone into a room and totally forgotten what you're doing there? If this sounds familiar, you're not alone; experts suggest that more than half of all Americans experience this problem occasionally. It's not incipient dementia—just a lack of attention.

Each time you think about going into a room to get something, simply stop for a moment and tell yourself what you're going to retrieve. If you're already in the other room and can't remember what you're doing there, try retracing your steps to where you were standing when you had the thought to leave the room. This form of association will often help jog your memory.

Remembering Places

If you lose your way as you walk or travel, you need to improve your memory of the directions as you go. Follow these important suggestions and you'll find that your memory for places improves dramatically:

- As you travel, pay attention to mental images you pass. Flash back to them in your mind once in a while.

- Record visual "cues" from both directions (things might look different when you return). Look for that big red barn, the funny sign, the crooked tree.

- Use all your senses. Pay attention to unusual smells or noises; the more senses you involve, the stronger the memory trace will be.

- Use maps. If you're not good at reading maps, write down directions and study them thoroughly before you leave home.

Remembering Quantities

If you've ever been in the midst of baking brownies and suddenly realized you had no idea of how much flour you've just dumped in the bowl, you need help in paying attention to *amounts.*

Try visualizing the amount of flour in the measure. Pour it in while saying aloud the amount you're using. "*One* cup . . . *two* cups . . ." You'll find that when you comment out loud on how many cups you've put in, you're less likely to forget or get sidetracked.

You may want to resort to a backup strategy. For every cup of flour you pour, set aside an object to represent that cup: a coffee bean, a raisin, a spoon. Each time you add another cup of flour, set aside another bean, raisin, or spoon. This way you can visually check exactly how much you've added, even if you're continually interrupted.

Remembering Short Lists

The most basic strategy for remembering is called the link method, a particularly good way to memorize short lists. It's a form of visualizing, but with this system you must link the items together by thinking of images that connect them. Here's how it works:

1. First, form a visual image for each item on the list.

2. Associate the image for the first item with the image for the second, then link the second with the third, and so on.

3. To recall the list, begin with the first item and proceed in order as each item leads to the next one.

4. When using the link system, don't try to associate every item with *every* other item, just associate the two items at a time.

While a grocery list does not necessarily have to be remembered in order (although it sometimes helps to find things faster), let's use it as an example:

corn

peas

apples

orange juice

buns

1. Form a visual association between the corn and the peas. Perhaps an ear of corn could be sitting on a porch shelling a bucket of peas. Dress the corn in a straw hat.

2. Next, create a link between the peas and the apples. Imagine one pea pod dressed like Carmen Miranda dancing with an apple wearing an evening gown and a tiara.

3. Now imagine the apple tripping over its gown and falling into a puddle of orange juice, where it is assisted by a bun flinging itself down into the juice.

When you're creating images, make them really vivid as you think of them. Of course, a creative, silly, or unusual link association is fine, but what's really important is that you use the first association that springs to your mind, since this will make it easier for you to remember the same association next time.

Take a few minutes to practice linking this bigger list of words. You may find that bizarre and wild associations are easy to remember:

saddle

piano

toad

paper

bird

truck

book

cat

sandwich

flower

football

window

radio

rabbit

fork

lips

sofa

hotel

How many could you successfully remember?

The problem with this strategy, of course, is that each link is associated with the one before it—except for the very first one. You have to be able to remember the first item on your own, and if you have a *really* bad memory, that could be a problem. To be safe, you should cue the first item in some way. If you're trying to remember a grocery shopping list, then link the first item with the front door of the store. In the grocery list given previously, imagine a big ear of corn lounging by the store entryway next to the grocery carts—or riding *in* a grocery cart.

The nice thing about the link system is that once you are good at using it to remember a few items, you can move on to remember twenty or thirty items—there's really no limit to the number of things you can remember with this system.

Again, if you have a really bad memory, it's possible that if you forget one item on the linked list, it may drag an item linked next to it into oblivion, too. If this is your problem, you can try the "method of loci" (we'll discuss this more fully in the next chapter), which works as follows:

Briefly, you begin by imagining your house or a building you know well. Simply link one item on your list with the front door. Then move into the entry and place the second item in the entry. Move around the house room by room, placing objects in the room. All you need to do to recall your list is to go to your front door, and the object will appear.

For example, to remember to buy batteries and cat food, simply envision your front door with a giant Eveready battery dressed in a nightgown leaning against the doorjamb. Open the door and find a giant cat food can sitting on your stairs, juggling some colored balls. Make each item memorable and you won't forget it. This method has an advantage over the link method: even if you forget one item, it won't affect your memory for the next one because all the items are linked to a place, not to one another.

Total Recall

Have a friend give you a list of twenty nouns (no verbs or adjectives). Write down each noun as it's called out. Associate the first word with the person; if the first word is "hat," imagine the person wearing an outrageous hat. That's all it should take to get you started recalling the rest of the list. Ask the friend to cue you to recall the items after ten minutes.

Summary

You can strengthen your memory (and your brain) by living in an enriched environment filled with unusual sights, sounds, and smells, and by engaging in new or challenging activities. Anything that makes you think will improve your brain's function. In addition, you can boost memory by exercising it—practicing lots of riddles, puzzles, and other mind games.

Besides general brain exercises and stimulation, there are lots of memory tricks you can use to help you remember specific types of everyday things, such as returning a library book, keeping an important date, or finding where you parked your car. In general these tricks include paying attention, focusing and concentrating, repeating important details out loud, keeping one good calendar and a to-do list, and leaving reminders around the house. The link and place systems are good strategies to use for remembering items on a list.

To remember . . .

- Habitual tasks: link them to something else you do.

- Where you put something: pay attention and be consistent about where you leave it; attach a homing device if necessary.

- Where you parked: make a mental note, write a description, or attach a flag to the antenna of your car.

- Schedules: keep a calendar, write a list, cue attention with a safety pin on your sleeve or a sticky note in prominent places.

- Where you're going: pay attention, record visual cues, use maps.

- Quantities: count aloud as you cook, or use a marker to count out each measure.

- Short lists: use the link method.

SELF-TEST

To review what you've read, see how many of the questions you can answer without rereading the chapter.

1. What is one of the best ways to keep your memory sharp?

2. Why do puzzles and riddles help to strengthen the brain and memory?

3. What can you do to your environment to improve your memory

4. Name one thing that interferes with your ability to pay attention.

5. Name three things you can do to help minimize general forgetfulness.

6. Name three poor lifestyle choices that can interfere with your memory.

ANSWERS

1. Engage in mental exercise.

2. These types of games help reinforce connections between nerve cells.

3. Add as much color, interest, novelty, and challenge to your environment as possible.

4. stress, anxiety, depression, lack of concentration, medication, alcohol, smoking, lack of sleep

5. Enrich your brain with puzzles and challenging games, enrich your environment, practice visualization, work on paying attention, engage in a healthy lifestyle.

6. drinking alcohol or too much caffeine, smoking, not getting enough sleep, eating a poor diet, abusing drugs

its

?

4 Improving Your Study Methods

Objectives

In this chapter you will learn:

- the right and wrong way to study

- how to boost your memory with flash cards

- how to retain what you read

- how to study using mnemonic strategies

Kim was a hard worker and a fairly good student, but every time she sat down to take a test, her mind seemed to go blank. She'd spend the entire night before poring over the book—to no avail.

It's not that Kim isn't bright enough or that she can't read. The problem is that no one ever taught her how to study. She would just sit down and open her books in the vague hope that by cramming everything into her brain the night before, she would remember what she'd read. That's really like throwing a stack of notes into a drawer and hoping somehow you'll remember what's on those notes when it comes time to take the test in a week or two.

Just how poorly this system works was underscored in a recent study in which children were tested after a simple reading exercise. The researchers discovered that when the children read a story without having any strategies to remember what they'd read, the next day the youngsters were able to retain only about 20 percent. That means they were forgetting 80 percent of the story. But once they learned some of the fairly simple strategies discussed in this chapter, their retention rates reversed themselves. Suddenly they were remembering more than 80 percent of what they'd read.

To increase your awareness of the way in which you study, answer the following questions:

1. When you know you have a test coming up, do you wait until the night before to study?

   _____

2. When you're facing a unit test, do you start at the beginning of the chapter and read it straight through once, then figure you've studied enough?

   _____

3. You've got several tests scheduled on one day. How would you go about studying for all of them?

   _____
   _____
   _____
   _____

Sadly, most schools never teach students how to study or how to remember what they read. Some teachers even believe that mnemonic techniques are a kind of cheap parlor trick—or, even worse, that they're a form of "cheating" involving sleight of hand not available to other students. Despite the fact that research has found that these techniques can help students as young as fourth graders remember important information, many educators still have the idea that mnemonics are bad because they don't help a child understand what he reads.

Yet the fact is that a great deal of basic schoolwork involves rote learning. Anyone who has ever sat down to learn the multiplication tables or worked on addition facts with an elementary-age child understands the reality of rote learning. There is simply no other way to absorb certain facts other than by rote memorization.

Using techniques to speed up rote learning frees students to spend more time in creative analysis and discussion in more advanced educational tasks. Mnemonics don't replace a good education—but they can certainly enhance it. In fact, *how* you remember doesn't matter at all, as long as you *do* remember—and as long as you're not reading the answers off your wrist during the test.

But because too many schools don't teach proper study techniques, too many students go about the process in all the wrong ways. Most popular: trying to cram a month's worth of work into one late-night study session. Is it any wonder memory fails them on the day of the test?

This chapter discusses why poor study habits don't work and presents a range of methods to help students remember what they've read or learned so that studying will really pay off.

Here's a simple example of how a memory "trick" can make all the difference:

1. Read this number *just once:* **8305842917.**

2. Who is the president of the United States?

3. What is your address?

4. What was the number that you read in question one?

Most people will have no idea what that number was for two reasons: it's a long number that doesn't mean anything, and there were other questions that interfered with the encoding of the number.

Now read this number: **(830) 584-2917.**

Most people can recall the number immediately after reading it. Yet this ten-digit number is exactly the same as the first one. The number *itself* didn't change—what's different is that the *way* in which you learned the number made it much easier for your brain to grasp. By breaking up this number into "chunks," your brain can much more easily make sense of it and remember it.

Flash-Card Tricks

In much the same way as demonstrated by the preceding exercise, learning a few memory tricks can help you retain information in easily manageable ways. You may not even be aware that you're retaining more information until you sit down in front of the test and discover that the answers pop right into your brain.

Here's an example of the right and wrong ways to go about learning new information. Karen came home from third grade with an assignment from her teacher. She was to learn the math facts written on a "math-facts addition card." Yet the teacher's misguided attempt to teach her students a rote-learning technique was all wrong. Here's what was on the card Karen brought home:

$$3 + 1 = 4 \qquad 3 + 6 = 9$$
$$3 + 2 = 5 \qquad 3 + 7 = 10$$
$$3 + 3 = 6 \qquad 3 + 8 = 11$$
$$3 + 4 = 7 \qquad 3 + 9 = 12$$
$$3 + 5 = 8 \qquad 3 + 10 = 13$$

The teacher told Karen she must start at the top and learn each math fact in order. As soon as Karen missed a fact, she was to go back to the beginning and start again. In only a few tries, Karen was totally frustrated and in tears.

The teacher was quite right that rote learning was the key to this exercise—but the approach was all wrong. The first several numbers were quite easy for Karen, and the more she practiced them, the better she got. But requiring her to start at the top and work her way down each time, stopping as soon as she got one wrong and going all the way back to the beginning, meant that in reality what she was doing was repeating the first few facts that she already knew, but not getting nearly enough practice on the more difficult facts that she didn't yet know. The more she had to go back and repeat math facts she knew, the more frustrated she became. By the time she worked her way down to the fact she didn't know, she'd forgotten it again and had to start over.

Why? The facts she knew interfered with the memorization of the facts she didn't know.

Fortunately, Karen's mother knew something about memory tasks. First, she made up an individual flash card with one math fact on each card; the answer was on the back. It was obvious that Karen knew the first three equations, so when Karen got to 3 + 4 and didn't know the answer, her mother stopped and held up the answer:

$3 + 4 = 7$

Karen repeated it. Then her mother held up the 3 + 3 card, which Karen already knew well.

Then her mother flipped the 3 + 4 card again. Since it had been just a second ago that she'd seen it, Karen remembered the answer. Her mother repeated the 3 + 3 card, which Karen knew, and then flashed the 3 + 4. Again Karen remembered the answer.

After several more flips from one to the other, it was obvious that Karen knew both math facts well. Her mother then introduced the next card: 3 + 5.

By focusing on only one new math fact at a time and constantly reinforcing her memory, in only a few minutes Karen had memorized the entire list.

When learning any type of information with flash cards—such as musical notes, multiplication tables, or division facts—it's important to take things slowly. Include three or four easy cards and one hard one. As soon as the hard fact is firmly memorized, add in the next hard one, but also keep an easy one. The easy answers help reinforce a child's sense of mastery and avoid frustration. Gradually adding in the difficult cards give a child's memory the chance to encode new information without being overwhelmed.

Also remember that there is a limit to how long anyone can sit and work on flash cards. Once the brain gets tired, memory performance is going to deteriorate. Do not work more than fifteen minutes at a flash-card exercise; the younger the child, the shorter the practice time should be. Never yell at a child during this exercise. A child who is frustrated or upset will not be able to memorize anything.

PQRST Method: Retain What You Read

Many memory experts believe that the "PQRST method" is the best study technique because it helps students retrieve information from their memory. PQRST is a memory trick itself—it's an acronym that stands for:

- **P**review
- **Q**uestion
- **R**eview
- **S**tate
- **T**est

Here's how the method would work if you were preparing for a major test.

Preview

Objective: To get an overview of what the chapter is all about. This should not take more than a few minutes. Here's how:

1. Read the chapter summary (at the end of a chapter) first. This will help you recognize the main points of the chapter as you read along.
2. Read the preface.
3. Read any table of contents for that chapter.
4. If the book provides an outline of the chapter at the beginning, read over this.
5. Now skim the chapter, especially headings, photos, graphs, and charts.

Completing this overview will give you a really good general idea of what is covered in the chapter. Want to see how this works? Try the following example.

To understand how a good preview can help you understand information, read the following paragraph:

> The procedure is really easy. You've got to get a lot of things together at once. It's important not to overdo things. Just do the

right amount. You may have to go somewhere else for the proper facilities: Be sure to bring the right supplies. The proper sequence must be followed, or things won't work out. After the procedure is completed, everything can be put back into its proper place. However, soon the cycle will have to be repeated.

Is it hard to figure out what's going on? Go back and read the paragraph again with the understanding that it is a description about taking a bath. Once you understand the concept, the entire passage makes far more sense. It's like that with previews, too.

Question

Asking yourself questions is an excellent way to remember information. Some textbooks include review questions at the end of a chapter. If your textbook has these questions, read these *first*—before reading the chapter. They will help focus your attention on the important points.

Now, as you begin, ask yourself questions as you go along. "Who is involved?" "Who is the king/president/bad guy?" "Why did that happen?"

Read over paragraph headings and ask yourself questions about them, too.

Read

Now read the chapter completely, *without* taking notes. The first time you read a chapter, *do not underline. Do not take notes.* Even for veteran studiers it's hard to pick out important points the first time around. Most people tend to underline far too much, just as they tend to take far too many notes. Don't fall into this trap!

1. Read one section without underlining.

2. Go back and, as you work your way through the paragraph again, underline the important points. *Think* about the points you are underlining.

3. Read the next section without underlining.

4. Go back and read the next section again, this time underlining.

State

Now reread the chapter and state the answers to key questions out loud. Ask yourself questions as you go and *answer* them—out loud. Don't worry about what your roommate might think! You should spend about half of your study time stating information out loud.

Test

Now for the fun part—test yourself to see if you have retained the information.

1. Go through the chapter again.

2. Ask yourself questions.

Space out this part of your studying so that you test yourself during a study session, after a study session, and right before a test. Remember, testing yourself right before a test is not "cramming"—that implies you've never seen the information before and you're trying to cram it into your head.

Done correctly, testing and retesting yourself is simply an effective way of reviewing information before the exam.

The PQRST method is a time-honored way of learning effectively. But there are other things to keep in mind that can help you record, retain, and retrieve information very effectively! Remember that studying is an active experience. The more you can do to make it funny, unusual, creative, or different, the more you will remember what you've studied.

What is the PQRST method?

Answer: The PQRST method stands for "Preview, Question, Read, State, and Test."

Make It Memorable

When it comes to remembering something, the more memorable an event, the easier it is to remember.

1. Think back to four days ago. What did you eat for lunch?

   _____

   _____

2. Think back to two weeks ago. What did you watch on TV?

   _____

   _____

3. Think back to your last birthday. Do you remember what you did?

   _____

   _____

The more emotional impact the information has, the more you will remember. This is why everyone remembers exactly where he or she was on September 11, 2001—but almost none of us would remember what we'd done the day before. It simply doesn't carry the same emotional weight. So, by making what you read memorable, you'll be better able to remember it. Here are some suggestions:

- Make note of what interests you in a chapter. Take a moment to make a mental comment—out loud if possible.

- Ask yourself what would happen in the chapter if one fact or event were different.

- Train yourself to summarize one section at a time. Read the section, close your eyes, and summarize it in a sentence. What are the logical conclusions or ramifications?

Visualize!

The more clearly you picture something in your mind, the better able you will be to remember it. If you're reading a chapter about the French Revolution, don't just read the words. Place yourself in the action. Smell the air—is it hot and dusty? Dry and cold? Include yourself in the images as you read. Imagine that you're standing by the guillotine and listening to the crowd. If you're reading about Marie Antoinette, imagine the peasants crowding into the palace to watch the royal family eat. What is the royal family like? What kind of food are they eating?

The better you are at putting yourself into the story, the better you'll remember what you read. Some people are naturally gifted at visualizing, while others have to work at it. However, when it comes time to take the test, the other students may have read the material—but you will have been there!

Let's suppose you're studying ancient Pompeii. Try the following exercises:

- Imagine the smell of the air.

- Smell the wine, the olive oil, the bread baking.

- Listen to dogs barking.

- Listen to the street sounds. Do you hear wooden carts creaking along the road?

- Now imagine the cloud of ash beginning to fall as Vesuvius erupts. What are the tastes, sounds, smells, feelings?

Obviously, it's much easier to place yourself into the social lives of ancient civilizations than it is to try to get interested in the major exports of Bolivia. If that's what you're reading about, don't sit there and try to memorize a long list of products: beef, wool, llama. Get creative and visualize! Imagine you're a Bolivian farmer raising llamas and cabbages. These techniques work well with any subject except those involving dates and numbers.

Acrostics

As you learned in Chapter 2, an acrostic is a mnemonic phrase created by linking the first letters of a series of words. If you were a young medical student, one of the most familiar would be this one: On Old Olympus's Towering Top A Famous Vocal German Viewed Some Hops.

What does it mean? The first letter of each of the words in this phrase stands for the first letter of each of the cranial nerves, in order: olfactory nerve (I), optic nerve (II), oculomotor nerve (III), trochlear nerve (IV), trigeminal nerve (V), abducens nerve (VI), facial nerve

(VII), vestibulocochlear nerve (VIII), glossopharyngeal nerve (IX), vagus nerve (X), spinal accessory nerve (XI), hypoglossal nerve (XII).

Test yourself:

Name the order of the planets in our solar system.

To remember the planets of the solar system in order, recall this phrase: May Vanna Earn Money Just Singing Until Next Payday? (Mercury, Venus, Earth, Mars, Jupiter, Saturn, Uranus, Neptune, Pluto. Note: You can remember that "May" stands for Mercury and not Mars because it ends in *y*, just as Mercury does).

Take a Note!

There are lots of students out there who may be dedicated note takers but who get to the test and still can't remember what they've written in their notes. This is because far too many students take notes in all the wrong ways.

How do you take notes? After you answer, read on to see if you're taking notes the best way.

- I listen very carefully to what the teacher says and write down everything word for word.

- I try to write down as much as I can, but I have trouble reading my handwriting later.

- I summarize only the main points the teacher makes.

As you may have guessed, there's a right and a wrong way to take notes.

WRONG: Writing down every single word the teacher says or that you read, word for word, without thinking of the content of the message. If you're so busy taking down every word, odds are you aren't *listening* to what's being said. This is why it's so hard to interpret notes later when you review them. It may seem odd, but it's possible to take perfect dictation and not really "hear" a thing.

RIGHT: Listening to your teacher and summarizing *in your own words* what's being said. Jot that down. Isolate what's important and don't waste time capturing each pearl of wisdom. Be a discriminating note taker.

Practice taking notes by watching your favorite TV show. Grab a pen and jot down what you hear on the show—but *summarize!* Trying to keep up with a fast-talking TV host will turn you into a discriminating note taker. Train yourself to listen *first* and then, when the speaker pauses for breath at a logical break, jot down a few key phrases that sum up what was said. If you're writing down every word, you're doing it wrong.

When to Study

If you want to remember what you read, *when* you study is just about as important as *how* you study. If you know you have a test on Friday, don't wait until Thursday night to work on these techniques. Start at the beginning of the week, on Monday, and schedule three or four short study sessions during the week. Try to use different study methods each time while you're learning the information. Your calendar should look like this:

Monday: Review chapter—PQRST.
Tuesday: Take notes.
Wednesday: Outline.
Thursday: Discuss material with classmate.

How you manage your time is also important. Too many students tend to spend more time on easier material and less time on harder work. In order to get the most out of your study time, you have to be able to assess the difficulty of the material that you need to remember.

First of all, it's a good idea to schedule a regular time to study. And remember, it's better to study for a test in three separate one-hour sessions than in one marathon three-hour session. While ultimately the same amount of time is spent studying, spacing out study sessions helps you better retain the information. This is probably because the mind can concentrate for only a certain amount of time.

You should also set specific goals about what you want to achieve during your study time. But don't set a specific amount of time as a goal: "I'll spend one hour reading social studies." Instead, make your goals subject-oriented: You'll get through a chapter, or a section in a unit. To work on your time-management skills, it's helpful to keep a log of your activities so you can tell how long it typically takes you to study material.

Study Log						
	Monday	**Tuesday**	**Wednesday**	**Thursday**	**Friday**	**Weekend**
Math						
History						
Science						
Language						
Reading						
English						
Other						
Other						
Other						

When should you start studying for a test on Friday?

Answer: The Monday before, at the very latest.

Don't Interfere

Jill and Elaine were college roommates, and both had a French final on Friday. After Jill finished her study session on Thursday night, she sat down at her computer and worked on a German term paper. Then she leafed through some fashion magazines while watching her favorite TV show. Right before bed she got out her economics textbook and read over the assignment. Elaine simply studied for her French final and then went to bed.

When the two compared notes the next morning over bagels, it was obvious that Elaine had a much better grasp of the material. The reason? Jill had allowed too many distractions to interfere with her French studies—especially by working on a different foreign language after she'd studied French. Research shows that the best way to do well on a test is to sleep right after studying. Elaine had allowed no other distractions to interfere with what she'd reviewed for her French final.

The more activities you engage in between studying for one subject and taking a test, the more they will interfere with how well you can remember the information. For example, if you spend three hours studying Latin before a test, you shouldn't then study Greek, because the similarity of the information will interfere with how well you can distinguish between the two.

This is why it's best *not* to study two similar subjects in the same location. Studying pathology in the kitchen and pharmacology in the living room will help you keep the two subjects separate in your mind.

What is one of the best ways to ensure that you'll do well on a test?

Answer: Go to sleep right after studying.

Method of Loci

The oldest known mnemonic strategy is called the **method of loci** (*loci* is Latin for "places"). It's based on the assumption that you can best remember places you're familiar with, so if you can link something you need to remember with a place you know well, the location will serve as a memory clue. We discussed this method briefly in Chapter 3 as a way of remembering lists.

According to the ancient Roman Cicero, this method was developed by the poet Simonides of Ceos, who was the only survivor of a building collapse during a dinner he attended. Simonides was able to identify the dead, who were crushed beyond recognition, by remembering where the guests had been sitting. This made him realize that it would be possible to remember anything by associating it with a mental location of a place. The loci system was used as a memory tool by both Greek and Roman orators, who took advantage of the technique to speak without notes. Dating back to about 500 B.C., it was the most popular system until about the mid-1600s, when the other mnemonic methods were introduced.

This method is especially effective if you're good at visualizing. Here's how it works:

1. Think of a place you know well, such as your own house.

2. Visualize a series of locations in the house in logical order. For example, begin at your front door, go through the hall, turn in to the living room, proceed through the dining room, into the kitchen, and so on. . . . As you enter each location, move logically and consistently in the same direction, from one side of the room to the other. Each piece of furniture could serve as an additional location.

3. Place each item that you want to remember at one of the locations.

4. When you want to remember the items, simply visualize your house and go through it room by room. Each item you associated with a place will spring to mind.

Here's how it would work if you wanted to remember the principal exports of Peru:

wool

iron

copper

lead

silver

cotton

coffee

At your front door, picture a big, fat, woolly sheep waving hello. Don't just see the sheep—really look at the wool. Get close and smell the lanolin. Then open the door and walk into the entry hall, where you see a tall five-iron golf club sitting on the stairs. Turn and walk into the living room, where a copper kettle is sitting on the sofa talking to a yellow lead pencil. Standing by the fireplace is a six-foot-tall silver fork holding a bale of cotton and drinking a cup of coffee.

Now when you sit down to take the test and need to recall the principal exports of Peru, all you need to do is approach your front door. Instantly the image of the sheep will pop into your mind. The more outrageous and unusual you make your images, the easier you'll find it is to remember them.

You can use this method for remembering lists of items or to recall important points during a speech, lists of names, things to do—even a thought you want to keep in mind. The method works well because it changes the way you remember, so that you use familiar locations to cue yourself about things. Since the locations are organized in a natural order that you know well, one memory flows into the next very easily.

You can adapt this system by adding other locations—your office building, a mall, your friend's house, a trip through your town, your garden—any place you know well. It doesn't matter how close or how far apart each room or landmark is. What *is* important is how distinct one place is from another. In other words, you might not want to use your town library, which very likely contains identical rooms filled with books. In addition to making each site very distinct and memorable, you'll want to be sure to have an association between an item and its location by having the item and location interact.

For example, if you were trying to remember the First Amendment and visualized a reporter just standing beside the desk in your front hall, it would not be as memorable as it would be if the reporter was busy typing the Constitution at the desk in your front hall.

When you use the method of loci, it's important to form a strong association between each item and its location. Have the item interact with the location in a compelling way.

You can also place more than one item in any location. If you have a list of fifty items to remember, you could place five items at each of ten locations. Each of these five items should interact at its location.

Link Method

This is one of the simplest of all the mnemonic strategies, and we discussed it briefly in Chapter 3 as a way of remembering lists. With this method you can simply memorize items by linking them one to the next.

1. Form a visual image for each item.

2. Associate the first image with the next one on the list.

3. Associate the image for the second item with the third, and so on.

4. When remembering, simply start with the first item and proceed in order as each item leads to the next.

Scientists have found that people who use the link or loci method can remember up to three times as many things as can those trying to remember without using the methods. These methods are more effective than the use of imagery or rehearsal alone.

Now practice the link method. Take a few minutes to practice linking this list of words. You may find that bizarre and wild associations are easiest to remember.

horse

viola

pig

book

pen

car

desk

house

dress

bagel

How many did you remember?

Remembering One Item Using Link or Loci

Both the link and the loci methods allow you to remember items, but neither lets you locate just one particular item. For example, if you wanted to find the tenth item on that list using the link system, you'd have to work your way down the first nine items to get it. Of course, this is true for anything we learn in a serial way—most people wouldn't be able to name the nineteenth letter of the alphabet without counting through from A to S.

One way around this problem is to place a distinguishing mark at every fifth place. Using the loci method, at every fifth place you could picture a five-dollar bill. At the tenth location visualize a clock with its hands pointing to 10:00 P.M.

The same thing can be done with linking. Link a five-dollar bill between the fourth and sixth items, for example, or a ten-dollar bill between the ninth and eleventh. With these additional strategies, there is really no limit to the number of things you can remember using those two methods.

Now take the same list as the one you memorized above—except this time link a five-dollar bill between the book and the pen.

horse

viola

pig

book

$5

pen

car

desk

house

dress

bagel

Now try to automatically remember the fourth item. It's much easier!

Story System

A close cousin to the link method is the story system, in which you link the items you want to remember in a story. Using the previous Peru products list, you could create a story like this:

"The furious sheep was so angry that she picked up an iron bar to throw at the sputtering copper kettle, who slipped on a lead pencil and landed on a silver plate. . . ."

You can see that the story system, unlike the link system, links all the items in an integrated narrative. This makes it much easier for people to remember all the items, since they occur in a linked framework, instead of an unrelated association of pairs.

On the other hand, it takes time and creativity in order to fit all the items into such a narrative. Some people just aren't good at making up stories, and even those who *are* find it difficult to create a memorable narrative with more than a few items to remember—the story grows complex quite quickly. The nice thing about the link method is that it doesn't really matter how long the list is. Further, the story method makes it hard to recall items out of sequence.

Scientists say that both methods can help you learn and remember lists of individual items. The link and loci systems can help you remember lots of different kinds of information, while the story method is very effective if you're trying to remember concrete words. All three systems are more effective than either rehearsal or imagery alone.

Again, using the same list as above, try to come up with a story that links each item with the next one:

horse

viola

pig

book

pen

car

desk

house

dress

bagel

Peg Systems

Peg systems are probably the best known of all memory systems, in which items are "pegged" to (associated with) certain images in a pre-arranged order. The method has been traced to the mid-1600s, when it was developed by Cambridge professor Henry Herdson, who linked a digit with any one of several objects that resembled the number (for example, 1—candle). The system gets its name from the fact that the peg words act as mental "pegs" on which you can hang the information that you need to remember.

The peg method is a bit more difficult, but unlike either the link or the loci method, it's not dependent on sequential retrieval. You can access any item on the list without having to work your way through the whole thing. It is, however, more complicated to learn at first. In the peg system you learn a standard set of peg words and then you link the items you need to remember with the pegs.

The peg method also can be used to help form concepts in tasks requiring high memory demands, in remembering ideas, and in similar applications. Peg words are helpful in remembering lists for shopping or errands and in organizing activities.

A number of different systems use a concrete object to represent each number. What's different is how you choose the object that represents each number. The systems include the look-alike method, the rhyming method, and the meaning method. Most peg systems don't include a peg word for "zero," but allow you to invent your own.

Rhyming Pegs (visual pegs)

The best known of the peg systems is the rhyming peg method in which numbers from one to ten are associated with rhymes: one-bun, two-shoe, and so on. This system was introduced in England about 1879 by memory expert John Sambrook. It's easy to use, and many people already know many of the pairs from the nursery rhyme "one, two, buckle my shoe." In order to use the system, you must memorize the words that rhyme with numbers one through ten:

1 = bun
2 = shoe
3 = tree
4 = door
5 = hive
6 = sticks
7 = heaven
8 = gate
9 = vine
10 = hen

1. As you say each rhyme, visualize the item that the peg word represents. Picture it vividly—is the bun a hot dog bun or a hot cross bun? Is the shoe a battered old sneaker or a black spike heel?

2. Now draw the item. The act of drawing will help you remember the rhyme, creating a strong mental association between the numbers and the words that rhyme with them.

3. Imagine each peg word as vividly as possible. By visualizing the object that each word represents, you'll fix it securely in your mind, creating a strong mental association between the number and the words that rhyme with them.

4. Once you've formed an association between the numbers and the words that rhyme with them, you've constructed your pegs. Practice by saying each of the peg words out loud.

5. Now try seeing the peg words for numbers as you jump around— five, three, one, eight. Because the words rhyme with the numbers, you don't have to say the numbers to remember the words.

If you want to remember a list, all you have to do is link each item with a peg—the first item with a bun, the second with a shoe, and so on. To remember the list, just call up the pegs, and the mental images linked to the pegs will be recalled automatically.

If you had a list of countries to remember—such as France, Italy, England, and Russia—you could start out (one) visualizing a Frenchman in a beret balancing a *bun* on his head. Then (two) imagine a muddy Italian loafer (*shoe*) squashing a piece of pasta. Then (three) think of a *tree* filled with English pound notes dangling in the breeze. Finally, (four) think of a bottle of vodka in a Russian fur hat banging on a *door* to be let in. Now when you think of one—bun—you'll think of France. Two—shoe—you'll remember Italy.

Peg words can help you remember lists of items. However, this method may not work for those with memory problems caused by brain damage on one side of the brain, since it requires remembering in two distinct stages, one involving the right hemisphere and the other involving the left.

Using the peg method, try memorizing the list of the planets in the solar system in order:

Mercury

Venus

Earth

Mars

Jupiter

Saturn

Uranus

Neptune

Pluto

Link each planet with the corresponding peg.

Phonetic Peg System

This version of the peg system is more flexible than the rhyming system but it's also more complex to use. It's also called a "number to sound" system, and that's exactly what it is—it relies on the relationship between numbers and their phonetic sounds: "0" is remembered as *z* (the first letter in "zero"); 1 is remembered as *t* or *d* (a written *t* has "1" downstroke).

In addition, each sound is also remembered as a word: 1 (*t*) is also remembered as "ties," and 2 (*n*) is remembered as "Noah." Note that in this system it's the consonant *sound* that matters, not the consonant itself. This is important, since the same letter can have different sounds.

While many people think that the phonetic peg system is too clunky and difficult to bother with, it has been used successfully with brain-damaged patients trying to improve their memory. Here's a list of consonant sounds for the first ten:

1 = *t* (*t* has 1 downward stroke)

2 = *n* (2 downstrokes)

3 = *m* (3 downstrokes)

4 = *r* (last sound of the word "four")

5 = *v* (Roman numeral for 5 is *v*)

6 = *j* (phonetic sound *j*; remember that *j* looks like a 6)

7 = *k* (*k* is made of two 7s, back to back)

8 = *f* (*f* in script looks like an 8)

9 = *p* (*p* is the reverse image of 9)

0 = *z* (*z* is the first letter of zero)

Once you learn all the consonant sounds for each number, you can put any number into words to make them easier to learn. To construct a word, you assign a peg word that begins with the consonant represented by the number. Two-digit numbers are represented by a peg word that begins with the consonant sound representing the first number and ends with a consonant sound representing the second number.

1 = tag

2 = napkin

3 = mail

4 = rose

5 = lamb

6 = jar

7 = kitten

8 = fat

9 = pea

10 = toes

11 = tart

12 = tan

13 = tam

14 = tar

15 = toll

Alphabet Peg Systems

The alphabet makes a good memory system, since it has a natural order that every American knows. In order to make the letters concrete, each of them either rhymes with the letter of the alphabet it represents or has the letter as the initial sound of the word. The alphabet peg system might be: *a* = hay, *b* = bee, *c* = sea. Peg words can be created that rhyme with (or sound similar to) the letters of the alphabet they represent:

a = hay

b = bee

c = sea

d = deep

e = eve

f = effect

g = geology

h = age

i = eye

j = jay

k = quay

l = elm

m = Emma

n = end

o = open

p = pea

q = cue

r = art

s = essay

t = tea

u = you

v = veer

w = double you

x = exit

y = why

z = zebra

If you don't like the rhyming aspect of the peg-word alphabet system, you can come up with a list that doesn't rhyme but simply uses the same letter of the alphabet to begin each word. The only problem with this method is that most people don't automatically know the numeric equivalent of each letter, so individual items can't be retrieved as easily.

a = artichoke

b = bat

c = cake

d = dog

e = elephant

f = fireman

g = goat

h = horse

i = iron

j = jelly

k = kangaroo

l = llama

m = mouse

n = napkin

o = orange

p = pail

q = queen

r = rat

s = shoe

t = tank

u = umbrella

v = vase

w = wagon

x = xylophone

y = yarn

z = zebra

Once you have visualized each peg and linked it to a root letter, these images can then be linked to the things to be remembered. Continuing our mnemonic example of the names of planets, here's how to remember the lists: *a*—ace—mercury, an *ace* of spades having its temperature taken by a *mercury* thermometer . . . *b*—bee—Venus, a *bee* stinging a model of the *Venus* de Milo . . . and so on.

Peg the President

Using the alphabet pegs, try to remember the first ten presidents of the United States, in order:

George Washington

John Adams

Thomas Jefferson

James Madison

James Monroe

John Quincy Adams

Andrew Jackson

Martin Van Buren

William Harrison

John Tyler

Other Peg-Word Systems

You can also select peg words on the basis of meaning: one = me (there is only one "me"); three = pitchfork (three prongs); five = hand (five fingers). Unfortunately, this system is limited because it's hard to find good peg words to represent numbers beyond ten.

Research has found that people can use peg-word systems effectively to remember up to about forty words, which is why the peg-word system is a good choice if you need to remember lists of items.

Summary

There are many study techniques that can help students remember information they need to know. The PQRST method is a study technique that stands for:

- **P**review

- **Q**uestion

- **R**eview

- **S**tate

- **T**est

Other study tips include the following:

- Make information more memorable as you read to help retain it.

- Visualize as you read to help you remember what you've read.

- Take proper notes by writing down a summary of major points.

- Space out your study periods, and don't spend too much time during any one study period.

- Don't study two similar subjects back to back.

- There are several mnemonic strategies you can use to help you study:

    Method of loci: In this method you visualize a place with which you're familiar, and link something you need to remember with each room. The location serves as a clue to help you remember.

Link method: You link one item on a list of things to remember with the next one.

Story system: A close cousin to the link system, in this strategy you link the items you want to remember in the form of a story.

Peg systems: Items are "pegged" to (associated with) certain images in a prearranged order.

SELF-TEST

1. What does the *S* in the PQRST method stand for?

2. What are some of the best ways to go about studying for a test?

3. Name the four mnemonic methods.

4. Name the different types of peg systems.

ANSWERS

1. state

2. Visualize and make information more memorable as you read, take good notes, space out your study periods, study one subject and go right to bed, don't study two similar subjects back to back, and don't cram the night before.

3. method of loci, link method, story system, peg systems

4. rhyming, phonetic, and alphabet peg systems

5 Learning and Remembering Foreign Languages

In this chapter you will learn:

- the best ways to learn a new language
- how to use similarities between two languages
- the best mnemonics for learning a foreign language

Americans are notorious for being poor foreign-language students, but it doesn't have to be that way. All you have to do is learn a language in the correct way. All of us learned *one* language, so it's obvious that we *can* learn.

Whether you're involved in business that takes you to cities around the world or you're just interested in traveling abroad, learning at least the basics of another language is important. Even if you don't plan to step outside the boundaries of your home country, learning a language will strengthen the connections in your brain, improving your overall memory.

We learn our native language by being immersed in that language, listening to our family communicate every day. Instinctively, parents tend to speak to their infants in very similar ways, which are designed to help the child learn a language—using a higher tone of voice, emphasizing one- or two-word sentences.

"Do you want the *rattle?*" we ask an infant, dangling the rattle in front of the child's face. *"Rattle?"* The word is repeated, with emphasis.

"Do you want some *milk?*" Again, the operative word is emphasized and repeated. "Here's your *milk.*"

What's clear is that we don't teach our children how to speak by handing them a grammar book and asking them to write out boring sentences over and over. Children learn by hearing how the language is spoken on a daily basis.

In fact, it's this theory that Dr. Shinichi Suzuki developed in his highly successful music-instruction method for very young children. Suzuki reasoned that since babies learn their language by hearing good examples of speech and repeating what they hear, it would follow that a young child could learn music in the same way. With his method, parents play recordings of Suzuki songs over and over to a child, who is then taught by ear how to play one piece that he has just been hearing. No young Suzuki student is ever plunked down in front of a piece of music and asked to read the notes. That comes later.

The same techniques work well when learning a foreign language. The best way to learn and remember the language is to hear native speakers using the words—you can play tapes or videos of the language. In order to maintain memory for the vocabulary, you must experience the language out loud—otherwise your active vocabulary will shrink, although your passive understanding will remain.

Where to Start?

If you're just starting to learn a new language, it helps to look for similarities between the language you know and the one you're trying to learn. This will give you a basis on which to build your knowledge. For example, while English is derived from Anglo-Saxon roots, it shares many words with the Latin languages—French, Italian, Spanish, and Portuguese. For example, "papa" is *père* in French, *papa* in Italian, *padre* in Spanish, and *papa* in Portuguese.

Read the following French words and see if you can guess their English meanings:

1. *marcher*

2. *animal*

3. *gros*

4. *hamburger*

5. *serpent*

6. *bébé*

7. *bleu*

8. *orange*

Answers:

1. walk

2. animal

3. fat

4. hamburger

5. snake

6. baby

7. blue

8. orange

Tapes

Get a language tape and listen to it every day, practicing along with the tape. You can buy tapes specifically designed to teach the language or listen to taped books in the language you want to learn. Even if you don't fully understand the words, it's important to hear the tones and rhythms of the language.

Rent or buy videotapes of films made in that language and listen to the language while looking at the subtitles. Or tape a foreign-language instruction show on TV. There are excellent series geared for both children and adults. Concentrate. Don't do anything else while you're viewing or listening to the tapes. Or set your TV's closed captioning to the language you want to learn. Listen in English and read the captions in the foreign language.

Continuing Education

Take a continuing-education course so you can brush up on the grammar while practicing conversational skills with others. Often these courses are available both at high schools and at "open universities" and local colleges.

Native Speakers

Practice conversational skills with a foreign-exchange student or with a neighbor from another country. Never miss a chance to speak the language, no matter how brief. The more contact you have with the language, the better you will remember it. Keep in mind that people who move to a foreign country will even forget the vocabulary of their native language if they don't speak it for years.

Periodicals

Read newspapers, magazines, or books in the new language at least once a week (or as often as possible). Reading is one of the best ways to keep a language alive in your memory. Try to read without translating in your mind from the foreign language to your native language.

If you find adult foreign-language books too difficult, look in the kids' section of bookstores. There you can find a range of simple books with lots of pictures that can help you learn another language easily and painlessly.

Radio

Listen to the radio in the foreign language. If you don't have a local station that offers the language, invest in a shortwave radio. These radios pick up broadcasts in many languages throughout the world. Try to listen consistently.

Learning Vocabulary

One of the best mnemonics for learning vocabulary in a foreign language is the key-word strategy, which uses a two-step approach to memorization.

1. Take a foreign word and associate it with a key word.

2. Form a visual image connecting this key word with its English meaning. It's a good idea to reinforce this link by making the visualization of the two as funny or memorable as possible.

For example, here is a list of everyday French words together with possible key words:

- *homme* (man), pronounced "um"—Imagine a man who is trying to think of what to say "um . . . um . . . um . . ." Imagine a man stuttering the word "um" loudly, wearing a lampshade on his head.

- *nez* (nose), pronounced "nay"—Picture a horse with a huge nose, neighing. Picture him wearing a straw hat with a flower.

- *livre* (book), pronounced "leave-ruh"—Picture a book, leaving (walking out the door).

- *lunettes* (glasses), pronounced "loon-ets"—Imagine a loon wearing spectacles.

If you were taking a test of these words and a question on the test asked the meaning of *homme,* you could simply pronounce it to yourself ("um") and the image of a man stammering "um" should immediately come to mind. Likewise, if you were presented with a question asking you to translate "nose" into French, you would immediately picture the horse's nose, which would then trigger the memory of the word "neigh"—and ultimately *nez.*

Write a list of five vocabulary words you are trying to memorize. Come up with key words and link them with an image. Then try to recall them.

1. _____

2. _____

3. _____

4. _____

5. _____

By employing the basic equation of vocabulary and key word, you can easily memorize a large number of vocabulary words. Using your imagination and visualization techniques, you can learn a great many foreign words in a short period of time.

Of course, not all foreign words have an equivalent sound in English. For example, the French word for squirrel is *écureuil,* pronounced "egg-cure-oi" You could come close by creating a phrase like "egg cure—oy!" and imagining a squirrel mother giving her weak squirrel child an "egg cure—oy!" That image of the grimacing squirrel should get you close enough.

You can also use this technique with phrases. The French translation for "What's that?" is "*Qu'est-ce que c'est?*" (pronounced "kess-ka say?") You could link that to the English phrase "What's that?" this way: "What's that? What did Kesska say?"

Most people take a pocket translation guide along with them when they travel to a foreign country. But paging through a guide when you're trying to talk to the natives is awkward and time-consuming. Why not study your guide on the flight and try to memorize as many of the simple words as you can? You'll be amazed, using the key-word association system above, at how many words you can commit to memory.

Learning important items on a restaurant menu can really come in handy. Here's a list of common French menu terms, along with possible key-word links:

- *ail* (garlic), pronounced "eye"—You're peeling a huge clove of garlic and squirt a big drop in your **eye.**

- *canard* (duck), pronounced "cah-nard"—A giant duck throws a big **can, hard.**

- *crevette* (shrimp), pronounced "cruh-vet"—Picture a giant dancing shrimp on the beach wearing a **cravat.**

- *l'eau* (water), pronounced "low"—The water level at the lake is **low.**

- *gâteau* (cake), pronounced "gah-toe"—You carry a cake and trip on the **gate,** stubbing a **toe.**

- *glace* (ice cream), pronounced "glass"—You lick a scoop of lemon ice cream that's as clear as **glass.**

- *homard* (lobster), pronounced "um-ard"—Picture a lobster, **hum**ming **hard** under his breath in his tank.

- *jambon* (ham), pronounced "zham-bohn"—**jam** a **bone** into a big picnic ham.

- *lait* (milk), pronounced "lay"—**lay** down a bottle of milk for the baby.

- *lapin* (rabbit), pronounced "lah-pan"—Imagine a cute rabbit **lappin'** up a drink.

- *pois* (peas), pronounced "pwah"—Imagine throwing a punch—**pow!**—at a pea pod.

- *pommes* (apples), pronounced "pum"—I'm going to **pummel** you with apples.

- *poulet* (chicken), pronounced "poo-lay"—The chicken will **lay** a **poo**-ey, smelly egg.

Once you learn some basic vocabulary, you can combine several techniques to increase your knowledge. For example, once you learn that *pommes* on the above list means "apples," you can figure out what *pommes de terre* means on a menu—in French, the word *terre* is derived from the Latin word *terra* meaning "ground." Therefore, *pommes de terre* means "apples of the ground"—or potatoes.

Now check how well you learned some of the above terms.

1. The French word for cake is _____.

2. The French word for lobster is _____.

3. The French word for milk is _____.

4. The French word for water is _____.

Answers:

1. *gâteau*

2. *homard*

3. *lait*

4. *l'eau*

Here is a list of other French menu terms. See if you can come up with your own key-word strategies.

* *agneau* (lamb), pronounced "ahn-yoh":

* *banane* (banana), pronounced "buh-nahn":

* *bifteck* (steak), pronounced "bif-tek":

* *boeuf* (beef), pronounced "boof":

* *citron* (lemon), pronounced "see-trohn":

* *croque monsieur* (grilled cheese sandwich), pronounced "croak m'sieu":

* *mignon de filet* (filet mignon), pronounced "min-yohn duh fillay":

* *pamplemousse* (grapefruit), pronounced "pom-pluh-moose":

* *sandwich jambon* (ham sandwich), pronounced "sand-weetch zham-bohn":

Context

Always learn new words in context—this way you'll remember them better. Knowing an entire phrase in a foreign language—"*Où est la gare?*" ("Where is the train station?")—is much better than simply pointing and blurting "*Gare?*"

Therefore, learn the vocabulary word first, and then learn the phrase it fits into. By practicing the phrase over and over, you'll learn it much more quickly than you might think. It's even better to have a practice partner who can ask questions that you then answer—and vice versa.

Flash Cards

To reinforce simple vocabulary words, make flash cards with the foreign word on one side and the English word on the other. Use single words or basic phrases, and work on no more than six at a time. Say the words out loud.

Practice

Simple rehearsal is the best way to reinforce foreign vocabulary words. Remember, this is how you learned English as an infant—hearing the words over and over, then repeating them as your parents corrected your pronunciation. Only constant practice will keep the foreign terms and phrases in your active memory. Focus on what's important—if you're traveling for a vacation, you should emphasize simple present, past, and future tenses and leave out the more esoteric ones. If you have even less time to practice, focus on the present tense—you can get by with one tense.

ASL

Learning any foreign language is stimulating to the brain. If you *really* want to stimulate your brain, consider learning American Sign Language (ASL). With ASL, your hands are responsible for communication, which requires different parts of your brain to be involved in language creation. Sign language is as rich and complex as any language, and it requires you to integrate sensory information in place of more typical auditory associations.

Summary

The best way to remember the words of a foreign language is to practice constantly and to immerse yourself in the language as much as possible by listening to tapes, radio, TV, or movies and reading the language every day. This is the way you learned English from your parents, and it's the most natural way to learn another language, too.

When learning a foreign language, start by comparing it to English. What words are the same, or nearly so? Find as many words as you can that mimic English, and you're off to a good start.

When trying to memorize another language, use video- or audio-tapes, practice with native speakers, attend workshops or continuing-education courses, listen to foreign-language radio or TV, and read periodicals or books in the language.

The best mnemonic trick for learning vocabulary is the key-word strategy—take a foreign word and associate it with an English word. As you're learning vocabulary, put it in context—learn the word as part of a sentence. Try flash cards as another good way of practicing. The more you practice, the better.

SELF-TEST

1. How do we learn our native language?

2. *Nez* means _____.

3. *Lunettes* means _____.

4. What is the Spanish word for "papa"?

5. Name three ways you can practice a foreign language that will help improve your memory.

6. What is the best way to use a pocket translation guide?

7. What is the best way to reinforce vocabulary words?

8. What is the best way to learn vocabulary words?

ANSWERS

1. by being immersed in the language and listening to the family communicate each day

2. nose

3. glasses

4. *padre*

5. listening to video- or audiocassettes and radio or TV shows; reading periodicals or books; speaking with a native, taking classes

6. studying the guide on the flight and memorizing some of the simple words

7. practice

8. the key-word strategy

6 Remembering Names and Faces

In this chapter you will learn:

- visual techniques to help remember names
- verbal techniques to help remember names
- why we fail to remember names

You're at a business party, chatting with someone you've just met. A third person comes up and you're expected to make an introduction—but you can't remember the new person's name.

This scenario is certainly not unusual. Most of us can remember faces quite easily, even if we've met the person only once or twice. But when it comes to attaching a name to that face . . . well, that's another matter entirely. It's usually much easier to remember what we see than what we hear, because the memory of a face is a simple job of recognition, activating a part of the right brain that specializes in spatial configuration. But remembering a name requires the brain to activate two separate processes—**recognition** and **recall.** Recognition is much easier for the brain to accomplish, because it simply requires you to choose among a limited number of alternatives. Recalling (the name that goes with the remembered face) requires a far more complex mental process.

Here is the difference between the two tasks:

1. **Recall:** Who was the president of the United States during the Civil War?

2. **Recognition:** Who was president of the United States during the Civil War?

   a. Benjamin Franklin

   b. Abraham Lincoln

   c. John Quincy Adams

Visual Technique

Since most of us recognize a face more easily than we can remember the name that goes along with it, it makes sense to cue the person's name by linking it to something in the person's face. This visual technique makes it easy to recall just about anyone's name.

What you need to do is link the name with the face, locking the two together. Using a visual technique, there are three simple steps to get the name right every time:

1. Associate the name with something meaningful. That's easy if the name is Bales (two bales of hay). If it's something more difficult, like Sokoloff, think of a phrase: "Soak it all off."

2. Note distinctive features of the person's face.

3. Try to form a visual association between the face and the name. If you've just met Jill Brown, and she has very dark, distinctive eyes, picture those brown eyes as you say the name to yourself. If the name is more unusual (Sokoloff) try linking it in a more general way: "He's got cheese on his tie. He'll have to **soak it all off.**"

After you've done all you can to remember the name, you need to rehearse the name if you're going to remember it. Repeat the name to yourself again in about fifteen seconds. If you've met several people, repeat the names to yourself before the end of the event.

Using this three-step technique will work because you're forcing yourself to think about the person's name in a meaningful way. It may seem hard at first, but there's really no name that can't be broken down into a funny set of words or phrases and then linked to a face.

Obviously, some names are easy:

Plowfields

Parker

Cage

Trees

Others are more challenging:

Wickenheiser—wicked hazer

Wohlsen—wool sent

Watazychyn (pronounced "watta-zitch-in")—whattya-itchin'

Remembering names can be an important social skill; we all like to think that other people remember us. The ability to remember names of even slight acquaintances is a highly regarded skill.

What's in a Name

Here is a list of ten names. Think of a picture to illustrate each name and write it down below.

1. Kennedy _____

2. Alvord _____

3. Smith _____

4. Bush _____

5. Taylor _____

6. McGovern _____

7. Spencer _____

8. Kahn _____

9. Wallace _____

10. Menuhin _____

Verbal Technique

Unfortunately, the visual technique does have its drawbacks. Some people just don't have very distinctive faces, or you may use the same facial trait so many times that it becomes hard to remember different people. And, as mentioned before, some people are naturally good visualizers, but others find it extremely difficult to find a visual cue and link it to a name.

If the visual technique just doesn't seem workable to you, there is another good choice—the verbal method. Here's one easy way to remember a name when you first meet someone, using a simple verbal technique:

1. **Register** the person's name—pay attention!

2. **Repeat** the person's name to yourself.

3. **Comment** on the name to yourself.

4. **Use** the person's name out loud as soon as possible.

Here's how it works. Joan Harris enters a business meeting and greets Jim Buie, a colleague, who introduces her to Shannon Kennedy.

"Hi, Joan!" Jim says. "I'd like you to meet Shannon Kennedy." Joan concentrates hard during the introduction, looking Shannon directly in the eye. As she shakes hands, she repeats the name to herself—"Shannon Kennedy. Shannon Kennedy"—and comments on the name to herself—"Like the airport in Ireland . . ." Then she uses the name out loud.

"Well, Shannon, what did you think of the agenda today?"

Remember Me?

Here is a list of ten first names. What could you comment to yourself about each name to make it memorable?

1. Shawn _____

2. Kara _____

3. Sue _____

4. Henry _____

5. Jacob _____

6. Christopher _____

7. Juan _____

8. Jill _____

9. Paul _____

10. Caroline _____

Interestingly, names of *objects* appear to be recalled quite differently than are names of people. Most people seldom forget the names of objects, whereas names of individuals are often forgotten. It appears that memory for proper names is different from memory for common nouns.

Experts say that people forget a name because they haven't paid enough attention or rehearsed the name enough to register it, or because they were tense, preoccupied, or distracted as they heard the name. It is not clear, however, why proper names are organized differently from object names, or why the recall of names is particularly susceptible to age and stress.

Name Game

Here's another way to practice remembering names. Cut out from a magazine ten photos showing ten different people's faces. Give half to your partner. On your five photos write a name on the back (make up anything you like). Have your partner do the same. Now exchange photos and practice trying to associate the name with something distinctive about the person's face. Wait for about fifteen minutes and quiz each other on the names.

Summary

Remembering a face is easier than remembering a name, because *recognizing* a face is a simpler memory task than *recalling* a name to match the face.

You can link a name with a face using the visual technique. In this method you find an unusual characteristic in a person's face and link it with an aspect of his or her name.

In the verbal technique you simply pay attention when being introduced, repeat the person's name silently once or twice, and then immediately use the name when speaking with the person.

1. Remembering a face requires _____, whereas remembering a name requires _____.

2. Describe the visual technique in remembering a name and face.

3. After you've used the visual technique to remember a name and face, what should you do?

4. Which is remembered more easily, names of people or names of objects?

5. What is the reason that people forget a name?

ANSWERS

1. recognition, recall

2. Associate the name with something meaningful. Note distinctive features of the person's face. Form a visual association between the face and the name. Rehearse the name and then repeat it to yourself later.

3. **Register** the person's name—pay attention! **Repeat** the person's name to yourself. **Use** the person's name out loud as soon as possible.

4. names of objects

5. Experts say that people forget a name because they haven't paid enough attention or rehearsed the name enough to register it, or because they were tense, preoccupied, or distracted as they heard the name.

7 Remembering Numbers

Objectives

In this chapter you will learn:

- what makes numbers easier to remember

- memory strategies to help you remember numbers

- how to figure out any day of the week for any date in the year

Whether you're an astrophysicist or a lion tamer, numbers are important. Remembering numbers is one of the most critical types of daily memory tasks there is. In fact, all of us use numbers every day.

Whether it's a Social Security number, a telephone number, an address—or a license plate, price, or ID number—how well we can remember numbers is of vital importance. But because numbers are abstract, remembering them can be one of the most difficult of all memory tasks. In this chapter you'll learn how to remember any kind of number—short or long—and in any sequence.

You may have noticed that there are a few numbers most people don't seem to have any problem remembering, such as a phone number. There's usually a reason for this, and it has to do with how memorable the number is or whether it's structured in a way that makes it *easy* to remember.

Other numbers or dates may not be so easy. Susan got married late in life and always had a terrible time remembering whether her wedding anniversary fell on April 23 or 24. It didn't relate to anything else in her life.

She complained about her memory lag one day to her sister. "I never have trouble remembering *your* wedding day," Susan complained. "I can remember that you got married May eleventh, the month after I did, and the double ones seem to make it an easy date to remember. But I can't ever remember whether my anniversary is on April twenty-third or twenty-fourth."

Her sister came up with the solution: "Just remember that *both* our anniversaries fall on an odd date," she said. "Since you remember mine, you can always remember that the date is odd, and so yours is the twenty-third and not the twenty-fourth because we both got married on an odd-numbered day." From then on, Susan had no problem remembering her wedding anniversary.

This illustrates the importance of putting numbers in some kind of context if we expect to remember them. The date of April 23 alone meant nothing to Susan, but when she could link it to the fact that it was an odd number—the same as her sister's anniversary, which for some reason she *could* remember—she had a workable memory strategy.

How to Remember Numbers

The first time you encounter a number, your eyes register the individual digits. As this sensory information enters your brain, it's retained just long enough to be briefly recalled if needed. For example, if you hear a new telephone number, you can probably remember it long enough to dial it; five minutes later the information is gone. However, if you repeat the number over and over, or if there is a strong emotional or sensory component to the number, you may be able to retain the information as it's encoded in long-term memory.

If you are highly motivated to remember numbers, or if you have lots of practice in working with a certain type of number (such as if you're a cashier in a grocery store), they can be easier to remember. If you're not highly motivated, or if the number is just too long or unremarkable, you'll find that remembering digits is much easier by using one of the following memory techniques.

Test Your Memory for Numbers

This is a test of your working memory for numbers. You'll need another person to help you with the test, someone who can read out the numbers for you. The helper should read the first sequence of numbers one at a time, a second apart: 3 . . . 9 . . . 0 . . . 2 . . . 1. You then repeat the sequence. Then the helper reads the second sequence of numbers: 4 . . . 9 . . . 3 . . . 4 . . . 2. You repeat them.

Series of five numbers:

3 9 0 2 1

4 9 3 4 2

2 0 3 8 6

Series of five numbers to be repeated in reverse order:

3 8 9 4 2

8 3 7 5 4

7 3 8 2 3

Series of six numbers:

5 6 8 7 5 2

5 1 5 3 1 2

3 4 7 8 0 1

Series of six numbers to be repeated in reverse order:

1 5 0 7 8 7

1 0 1 4 0 5

0 6 4 1 5 2

Series of seven numbers:

8 2 9 6 9 5 5

6 7 9 5 8 3 0

8 4 0 8 4 5 6

Series of seven numbers to be repeated in reverse order:

7 2 7 0 1 9 5

6 5 1 6 3 7 4

9 6 8 2 5 1 0

Series of eight numbers:

5 8 4 6 2 0 8 6

2 7 9 7 4 0 1 8

6 4 9 7 1 1 2 0

Series of eight numbers to be repeated in reverse order:

7 4 9 8 0 1 5 4

2 7 5 0 7 0 9 3

5 1 9 6 8 3 3 2

Score

An average adult can repeat two out of three seven-number sequences.

An above-average adult can correctly repeat a sequence of eight numbers, and can correctly repeat, in reverse order, seven numbers.

Numerical Relationships

If there's some relationship among the digits in a number, it can be much easier to remember. While not all important numbers have identifiable relationships, many do. For example, in the license plate XYZ-2468 you can see that each number is two more than the one before. With the number 1,344, the first two digits add up to a four, which is repeated. Other numbers may be linked to dates. John remembers the last four digits of his Social Security number (1066) because that's when William the Conqueror conquered Britain. Sarah can remember her new phone number's last four digits (1776) because that's when the Declaration of Independence was signed. Jane had her first child on January 23, so she could easily remember the numerical translation of the date: 1/23.

Over the course of the next week, practice looking for memorable ways to remember numbers. The more you practice, the easier and more natural it will become. As you drive, look at license plates and try to find relationships among the digits. Get your kids into the act and challenge them to see relationships in numbers, too.

Chunking

One of the best ways to remember information is to use the chunking method; that is, to group separate bits of information into larger chunks in order to better remember them. Often, organizing them in a particular way, such as according to sound or rhythm, can help you recall them.

For example, if you want to remember a ten-digit phone number (9991357920), it's much easier to break it up into chunks of three, three, and four digits: (999) 135-7920. That's also why Social Security numbers are given in chunks of three-two-four (123-44-5678 instead of 123445678). Remembering things is easier when the information is grouped in smaller chunks. It helps to pause between the numbers, too.

Try this with other long numbers that are more unfamiliar, such as your checking-account number or a credit-card number.

Why is it easier to remember your phone number than a credit-card number?

Answer: The phone number is broken down into chunks of three numbers, three numbers, four numbers.

Visualize It

Just as with other types of information, visualizing can be a helpful way to remember numbers. This is especially useful if you are by nature a good "visualizer." Let's say you just witnessed a hit-and-run accident and got a good look at the offender's license-plate number—and you don't want to forget it before reporting it to the authorities. You could try simply repeating it to yourself over and over, but the odds are fairly high that you might not remember it.

In this case you might not have time to remind yourself to find a relationship among the individual digits or to chunk them. Instead, you could visualize the number—imagine it painted in big, fat, bright turquoise digits on a white picket fence. The actual color or location on which you visualize the number isn't important, but the brightness and clarity of the vision are critical. The more unusual the color or style, the more likely that you'll remember it. Think of the number written in a blazing comet tail streaking across the dark night sky, or encrusted with diamonds and rubies on a piece of black velvet.

As you visualize the number, say it out loud. In this way you're using several senses to encode the memory. An auditory clue will thus be linked with the visual memory, making retrieval more likely.

Barbara has a new dining room table and wants to buy some table-cloths to fit it. She measures carefully—it's just seventy-two inches long—and writes down the dimensions on a piece of paper. But by the time she gets to the store, the paper is missing. Every time she's at a department store and remembers she needs a tablecloth, she realizes she still doesn't have the paper with the dimensions written down.

Here's how she can remember the size of the tablecloth without needing to write it down: If the table is seventy-two inches long, she can simply envision a huge number "72" made out of bread rolls balanced on her dining room table. As Barbara envisions the rolls, she says to herself, "This table measures seventy-two. I wonder if I'll still be using this table when I'm seventy-two." It's a safe bet that when Barbara next finds herself in the tablecloth department, the vision of "72" will pop immediately into her mind.

Secret Code

There are other ways to remember numbers that may appeal to some people who like codes and mathematical puzzles. One of the best ways is to create words out of numbers. For example, to remember the number 142:

1. First give each number its numerical equivalent (that is, one is *a*, four is *d* and two is *b*.)

2. Now come up with a phrase or sentence made of words beginning with those letters: *adb* might stand for the phrase "**a dog bone.**"

3. Say it out loud and visualize the phrase to help you remember it.

4. To remember the numbers, simply remember the sentence, and transform the words' first letters back into numbers.

For practice, try these:

1. Find the letter equivalents for the number 385. Devise a phrase with words beginning with those letters. Repeat it out loud.

2. Find the letter equivalents for the number 2,948. Devise a phrase with the words beginning with those letters. Repeat it out loud.

3. Find the letter equivalents in the number 30,486. Devise a phrase with the words beginning with those letters. Repeat it out loud.

Phonetic Peg System

You can use the phonetic peg system that you learned about in Chapter 4 to remember numbers, although it's a bit cumbersome unless you've learned the list. Remember, with this system each number is translated into a corresponding letter or sound:

1 = *d* or *t*

2 = *n*

3 = *m*

4 = *r*

5 = *l*

6 = *sh* or *ch*

7 = *k*, hard *c*, or *g*

8 = *f, ph,* or *v*

9 = *p* or *b*

10 = *s* or *z*

Once you've memorized this list *really well*—well enough to be able to transpose a number into a letter—you're ready to use it to remember numbers. For example, if you want to remember your new colleague's phone number, you would first translate each number into its peg-word letter. You could then make a word or phrase out of the number. Remembering the word or phrase will give you the phone number.

Here's how it would work with the phone number 789-1234. After translating each number, you'd get the letters *cfbtnmr*

Now come up with a phrase: **c**ats **f**ind **b**ig **t**una **n**ear **m**y **r**oom.

You can see that in order for this method to work well, you've got to memorize the list perfectly.

Call It up

Try this method with the phone number 945-1076. Now try it with your own phone number.

Visual Peg System

If you're more visual, you can try the visual peg system that you learned about in Chapter 2. Remember that in this system each number is matched to a picture that resembles the number:

1 = spear

2 = swan

3 = pitchfork

4 = sailboat

5 = spread-out hand

6 = snake

7 = gallows

8 = hourglass

9 = snail

0 = plate

To remember the Social Security number 365-82-4910, translate the numbers into the pictures and then visualize each picture:

pitchfork

snake

hand

hourglass

swan

sailboat

snail

spear

plate

Now link the words together: A pitchfork threatens a snake, just as a hand holding an hourglass snatches him out of the way and flings him over to a swan sailing a sailboat, who takes him aboard and seats him next to a snail carrying a spear and sitting on a dinner plate.

After you've memorized the visual-peg linking words, practice with your own Social Security number. Try to use the visual peg system to memorize it. Now try using a number you don't know well, such as your license-plate or a credit-card number.

Find Any Date

Here's a quick way to figure out any date in the year. Simply memorize the first Sunday in each of the twelve months. For 2003, the code would be January 5, February 2, March 2, April 6, May 4, June 1, July 6, August 3, September 7, October 5, November 2, and December 7 (or 522-641-637-527). Now you know that the first Sunday in January is January 5, the first Sunday in February is February 2, the first Sunday in December is December 7, and so on.

To find the day of the week for September 9, you see that the first Sunday is September 7. Simply count ahead by two days to find out that September 9 would be a Tuesday. To find the day of the week for September 30, simply add seven to get the second Sunday (September 14), and then add two more sevens to get to the fourth Sunday (September 28). Count ahead two days to arrive at September 30, which falls on a Tuesday.

Using the above technique, find the day of the week for these dates:

March 5, 2003
July 9, 2003
November 29, 2003

Summary

Numbers are initially registered for a fleeting second; only if you make a concentrated effort to encode the number into short- and then long-term memory will you be able to recall the numbers.

You can make numbers easier to remember by searching for a relationship between them or by "chunking" them, as in a telephone number. Strongly visualizing a number, in color on a white background, can help you to encode the memory. Peg systems are more intricate ways of translating numbers into letters and then words that can help you boost recall.

SELF-TEST

1. Why are numbers among the hardest things to remember?

2. What makes numbers easier to remember?

3. Name the memory strategies to help you remember numbers.

4. Describe the two peg systems.

5. Describe the system for figuring out any day of the week for any date in the year.

ANSWERS

1. because they are abstract

2. being highly motivated, working with the numbers a great deal, or learning memory strategies to help you remember

3. relationships, chunking, visualization, secret codes, peg systems

4. Visual pegs, in which each number is matched to a picture that resembles the number, and the number is then linked to the picture:

1 = spear
2 = swan
3 = pitchfork
4 = sailboat
5 = spread-out hand
6 = snake
7 = gallows
8 = hourglass
9 = snail
0 = plate

Verbal pegs, in which each number is translated into a corresponding letter or sound and then linked:

1 = *d* or *t*
2 = *n*
3 = *m*
4 = *r*
5 = *l*
6 = *sh* or *ch*
7 = *k,* hard *c,* or *g*
8 = *f, ph,* or *v*
9 = *p* or *b*
10 = *s* or *z*

5. Memorize the first Sunday in each of the twelve months. Then you can just add seven to get any successive Sunday and count from there to get the rest of the days of the week for the month.

8 Remembering Speeches

Objectives

In this chapter you will learn:

- why memorizing or reading a speech is the wrong approach
- how to use the link method to remember a speech
- how to use the loci method to remember a speech

There you are at your desk staring down at five pages of a speech you're supposed to give to your colleagues tomorrow night. You're trying to memorize the whole thing, but you're worried that when the time comes, you won't remember it. What should you do?

First, let's analyze your feelings of discomfort about giving speeches.

Take a few minutes to examine the following questions about you and your speeches. Completing this profile will help you uncover elements that may affect your performance before an audience.

1. When giving a speech, do you:
   - ❏ speak in a monotone?
   - ❏ speak from memory?
   - ❏ read your speech?
   - ❏ include jokes in the speech?
   - ❏ enjoy talking in front of others?
   - ❏ try to engage the audience in warm repartee?
   - ❏ just want to get it over with and flee the stage?

2. Have you ever:
   - ❏ forgotten key points in a speech?
   - ❏ lost your train of thought?
   - ❏ gotten sick before giving a speech?
   - ❏ felt frozen before having to give a speech?
   - ❏ avoided taking a job promotion because it involved speaking in front of others?

Wrong versus Right

Now that you've had a chance to think about your past speech experiences, it's time to learn the right and wrong ways of going about speaking in front of an audience—and how best to remember what you want to say.

First of all, *don't memorize*. A memorized speech doesn't sound like a spontaneous, off-the-cuff set of remarks—it sounds canned. Even Jay Leno would probably sound boring if he recited a memorized speech. What's worse, if you do try to memorize a speech and then forget a word or phrase, odds are you'll panic—and that will only lead to further memory problems.

Of course, you can sidestep this problem by reading your speech, but that's worse than memorizing it, because you'll be guaranteed to put your audience to sleep. And woe to you if you lose your place—more fumbling and panic.

The next time you give a speech, or hear one, evaluate the performance.

1. Did the person read the speech in a monotone? What was the audience response?

2. Did the person recite the speech from memory, word for word?

3. How would you have done the speech differently to have improved audience interest?

Ideally, what you want to do is appear before your audience and calmly have a conversation with them, in your own words, just saying what you want to say. Sound impossible?

Not at all. The best speakers do this every day, using the same techniques that you can master. There are a whole range of mnemonic strategies you can use to help you remember a speech without having to learn the whole thing word for word, and without reading it from cue cards or index cards. What's a speech, anyway, but a series of thoughts strung together in an interesting way? If you can use your own words and follow a logical sequence, you'll be home free.

To do this, you'll have to write out the whole speech, to make sure you cover the important points. Next, you can simply choose one of the mnemonic techniques we discussed in earlier chapters.

Method of Loci

As you've already learned, one of the oldest ways of remembering a speech is to use the method of loci, in which you place information in imaginary locations. To remember the information, you remember the location. Here's how to remember a speech using this method:

1. Write down the main points of your speech.

2. Choose a familiar building in which to place the main points of your speech—your own home is a good choice.

3. Visualize the first point of your speech at your front door.

4. Visualize the second point of your speech in your entranceway.

5. Move through your home in a logical sequence, leaving one main point in each room.

6. When you stand up to give your speech, simply go to your front door—the first point will be waiting for you. Mentally work your way around the rooms and you'll have all the main points of your speech.

Practice how you might go about using the method of loci for a speech.

1. Find an interesting magazine article and read it thoroughly.

2. Go back and underline the key thought in each paragraph.

3. Now take each key thought and place it in each location in your building.

4. Now stand up before a mirror and practice going through your house, recalling each key thought. Deliver the article as if it were a speech.

Link Method

Of course, the loci system isn't the only way to remember a speech. You can use a different mnemonic strategy if you prefer. Some people prefer the link system to remember the main points in a speech, selecting a key word to represent a whole thought and then linking those words.

The link system will help you remember things in sequence, which is all you really need to do with a speech. If you can remember each topic, you can use your own words, as long as you're going through the speech in a logical manner.

First, you'll need to write out the entire speech. Read over the speech, making sure you've included all the ideas you think are important. Next, select a key word that will remind you of an entire thought. It will be these key words that you link, one to the next. Now go back over your speech and underline each key thought.

Let's say you're giving a speech on how to write a nonfiction article. You've written out your speech and underlined all your key thoughts:

Find a market
Query letter
Contract
Research
Writing

Your first key thought is the word "market," which you can change into some silly image, such as "Mark et (ate)." Then you would link the idea of "Mark 'etting' " to "query letter"—a "queer letter."

The next key word is "contract"; continue the link, seeing "Mark etting a queer letter" that turned out to be his contract. Envision the contract all crumpled up and half eaten. Next, link "contract" to "research" a book he was "writing." Thinking of the first thought— "Mark etting" will remind you of the first key thought in your speech, which you can talk about in your own words, since you know the topic so well. When you've covered that topic fully, you'll automatically be reminded that "Mark et the queer letter," which will remind you of the entire thought—to discuss query letters. And so on you can go to the end of the speech.

If you want to link smaller thoughts (such as "what to put in a query letter"), you can do this simply by forming more links to the "queer letter" idea. While you're giving your talk, you can easily think of your offshoot link, and you'll still be reminded of the next thought you originally associated to "queer letter."

Once you know the sequence of thoughts, the exact words in which you describe these thoughts should not be a problem if you know the topic well. With this technique, you can also memorize song lyrics, jokes and punch lines, and play scripts.

Practice how you might go about using the link method for a speech.

1. Find another interesting magazine article and read it thoroughly.

2. Go back and underline the key thought in each paragraph.

3. Now take each key thought and make up a link to the next thought.

4. Now stand up before a mirror and practice going through the links, recalling each key thought. Deliver the article as if it were a speech.

Summary

A speech should never be memorized in its entirety or written out and read. Either way it's going to sound boring. Instead, you should pick out the key thoughts you want to cover and then practice a memory strategy to recall those thoughts. The actual words you use to describe the thoughts will be your own and need not be fixed. You can use either the method of loci or the link method to remember the key thoughts of the speech. These methods will also work to remember song lyrics, scripts, or jokes.

1. Why shouldn't you memorize a speech?

2. What's wrong with reading a speech?

3. What's the best way to give a speech?

4. Describe the method of loci as it would be used for a speech.

5. Describe the link method as it would be used to remember a speech.

6. Read the following speech and underline the key points:

> Four score and seven years ago our fathers brought forth upon this continent a new nation, conceived in liberty and dedicated to the proposition that all men are created equal. Now we are engaged in a great civil war, testing whether that nation or any nation so conceived and so dedicated can long endure. We are met on a great battlefield of that war. We have come to dedicate a portion of that field as a final resting-place for those who here gave their lives that that nation might live. It is altogether fitting and proper that we should do this. But in a larger sense, we cannot dedicate, we cannot consecrate, we cannot hallow this ground. The brave men, living and dead who struggled here have consecrated it far above our poor power to add or detract. The world will little note nor long remember what we say here, but it can never forget what they did here. It is for us the living rather to be dedicated here to the unfinished work which they who fought here have thus far so nobly advanced. It is rather for us to be here dedicated to the great task remaining before us—that from these honored dead we take increased devotion to that cause for which they gave the last full measure of devotion—that we here highly resolve that these dead

shall not have died in vain, that this nation under God shall have a new birth of freedom, and that government of the people, by the people, for the people shall not perish from the earth.

—Abraham Lincoln

ANSWERS

1. If you memorize your speech, it won't sound spontaneous—it will sound canned. And if you forget part of it, you'll panic.

2. Reading a speech is guaranteed to sound boring, and if you lose your place, you'll panic.

3. Use a memory strategy to recall key thoughts and describe them in your own words.

4. In the method of loci, you simply write down a key word in each main thought and place it in one of the rooms of your memory building. To recall the speech, you simply go to the front door and retrieve each key word.

5. In the link system, you choose a key word in each thought and then tie each word to the next by a funny, unusual link that tells a story.

6. There is no right answer. Everyone's key points will be different according to their own understanding of the material.

9 Maintaining Memory as You Age

Objectives

In this chapter you will learn:

- what's normal and what's abnormal about memory loss

- how the brain changes with age

- how to protect against memory loss as you age

- differentiating between Alzheimer's disease and normal forgetting

There you are at a school function, and you see another parent across the room. As you walk over, you suddenly realize you can't remember the person's name. Odds are that you're not suddenly developing Alzheimer's disease, although many people jump to that conclusion. You're simply experiencing a breakdown of the memory process that many of us begin to have trouble with in our twenties and that tends to get worse as we enter middle age.

No matter what you might have heard, memory loss is not an inevitable part of aging. In fact, while some memory loss is common as we get older, memory power typically diminishes only slightly as the years go by.

Take an inventory of the kinds of things you're liable to forget as you get older.

❑ names

❑ faces

❑ travel directions

❑ simple mathematical exercises

❑ difficult words

❑ easy words

❑ what you came into a room for

❑ where you placed your keys

❑ where you placed your glasses

❑ where you left the cordless phone or TV remote

❑ whether you took your medicine

❑ what you wanted to tell the doctor

❑ important appointments

❑ bills

This age-dependent loss of function appears in many animals, and it begins with the onset of sexual maturity. We saw earlier in this book that as you learn and remember, the connections between new cells change. Your synapses are reinforced and make more and stronger connections with each other. But as you age, these synapses begin to falter, which affects how easily you can retrieve memories.

As you get older, your attention span may get shorter, your thinking may slow down, and learning might take a bit longer. You'll probably maintain your short-term memory, your searching techniques, and retention of well-known information.

Researchers have several theories behind this deterioration, but most suspect that aging causes major cell loss in a tiny region at the front of the brain that leads to a drop in the production of a vital neurotransmitter called acetylcholine. Acetylcholine is important to learning and memory.

In addition, some parts of the brain vital to memory are highly vulnerable to aging. One area, called the hippocampus, loses 5 percent of its nerve cells with each passing decade beginning in your fifties—or a total loss of 20 percent by the time you reach your eighties. In addition, the brain itself shrinks and becomes less efficient as you age.

Of course, other things can happen to the brain to speed up this decline. You may have inherited some unhealthy genes, you might have been exposed to poisons, or perhaps you smoked or drank too much in your youth. All these things accelerate memory decline.

So you can see that as you age, some physical changes in the brain can make it more difficult to remember efficiently. The good news is that this doesn't mean that memory loss and dementia are inevitable. While some specific abilities do decline with age, *overall memory remains strong for most people throughout their seventies.* In fact, research shows that the average seventy-year-old performs as well on certain cognitive tests as do many twenty-year-olds—and many people in their sixties and seventies score significantly better in verbal intelligence than do younger people.

Evidence from animal studies suggests that stimulating the aging brain can stop cells from shrinking and can even increase brain size in some cases. Rats living in enriched environments with lots of toys and challenges have bigger brains composed of larger, healthier brain cells. Animals given a great deal of mental exercise have more dendrites, which allow their cells to communicate better with each other. Research has clearly shown that a stimulating environment encourages the growth of these dendrites and a dull environment impedes that growth. Studies also have indicated that many of the memory problems experienced by older people can be improved—or even reversed. You learned in Chapter 3 how to create an enriched environment to keep memory sharp. It's even more important for older folks to continue to upgrade their environment to make things interesting, challenging, and new.

Studies of nursing-home populations show that patients were able to make significant improvements in memory when given rewards and challenges. Physical exercise and mental stimulation also can really improve mental function.

It's clear that participating in intellectual activities can help ward off memory problems and even Alzheimer's disease. In one recent study, healthy subjects who did not have Alzheimer's were found to have been more active and intellectually stimulated between ages forty and sixty than had the patients with Alzheimer's. The researchers recorded participation in twenty-six activities, including television watching. (Of all the activities, only watching TV didn't seem to protect against Alzheimer's disease.)

So what does seem to work? Those pursuits that are creative and intellectual in nature—if you perform them regularly—really help protect memory:

- reading
- constructing jigsaw puzzles
- working crossword puzzles
- playing a musical instrument
- working on various crafts
- painting, drawing, or making other artwork
- doing woodworking projects
- writing letters
- playing card games
- playing board games such as checkers, chess, Monopoly, and Scrabble
- doing home repairs
- knitting or doing needlework
- gardening

Researchers suspect that by becoming involved with mind-stimulating pursuits people might build up activity in their brain cells that could later prove effective in protecting against memory disorders. As we learned in the first chapters, the brain is extremely plastic, and it responds well to stimulation. Nerve cells will grow or die depending on how much they are stimulated intellectually.

It's never too late to begin beefing up your intellectual pursuits—and this doesn't mean watching an extra few episodes of your favorite

TV show. Even if most of your life you've avoided museums, concerts, and libraries, it's never too late to begin.

In the last two weeks, have you:

❏ read a book?

❏ read a newspaper?

❏ worked a puzzle?

❏ done house repairs?

❏ worked in the garden?

❏ prepared a new recipe?

❏ taken a trip?

❏ visited or hosted friends?

❏ played a challenging game (such as chess)?

❏ learned a new skill?

❏ played a computer game?

Action Plan

After you've taken stock of what you have been doing, you may be surprised at how little you've been challenging your brain. If so, it's time to take the first step in changing your life. This action plan will help you move toward becoming more active—by writing down your goals toward making your life more adventurous or active. List your goals for what you would like to accomplish in the next month under the following headings:

New Tasks on the Job

_____

_____

_____

New Activity/Skill to Learn Per Month

_____

_____

_____

Weekly Exercise (walking, biking, etc.)

_____

_____

_____

Community/Charity Participation

_____

_____

_____

Family Activities

_____

_____

_____

Leisure Activities

_____

_____

_____

House Redecoration

_____

_____

_____

Now that you've got your goals for the month, do the best you can. If you fall short, don't beat yourself up. Just add those goals you haven't reached onto next month's plan. Keep in mind, you don't need to set goals under each category. Just choose a few that you think you might like to accomplish, and gradually add more categories as you feel you're making progress. Keep your goals realistic.

Lifestyle Changes

Reports about the rising tide of dementia may seem frightening, but the truth is that there are lots of things you can do to prevent memory loss. So now it's time to learn techniques to maintain or improve memory and reverse decline—simple changes you can make in your everyday life, such as getting more physical exercise and mental stimulation. We'll also discuss using "external aids" such as notes and diaries.

If you need to improve your memory for names or memorize a speech, you can simply read the appropriate sections of this book to learn specific techniques. They will work no matter how young or old you are.

For more general "memory boosting" for aging adults, one of the easiest ways to start improving your memory is to begin living a healthier lifestyle. Eating a good diet, minimizing stress, getting enough sleep, cutting down on alcohol and caffeine, and throwing away that last pack of cigarettes will all help improve your brain and memory function.

Exercise

Exercise can help you improve just about every aspect of your health, from boosting your cardiovascular fitness to preventing breast cancer. And now we know—surprise, surprise—that it can also help improve your memory. Studies have found that people who exercise frequently have a distinctive brain-wave pattern characterized by steep peaks and valleys (a factor associated with alertness). These high-exercise folks are better at blocking out distractions and focusing, which means that they're better at retrieving memories when needed. Research also has determined that aerobic exercise can help maintain short-term memory, especially as it applies to general and verbal memory. This type of memory is especially important when you want to recall names, directions, and telephone numbers or match a name with a face.

Aerobic exercise helps keep your heart strong and your blood vessels healthy and flexible, which means that your brain is getting plenty of oxygen and nutrients for optimum performance. This is important because, while only 2 percent of your weight is made up of brain cells, they use a fourth of all the sugar and oxygen your body absorbs. Research also suggests that exercise boosts a growth factor called brain-derived neurotropic factor that makes brain cells healthier.

Which of these memory-enhancing aerobic exercises do you regularly participate in? Aim for three times a week for thirty minutes of:

- swimming

- cycling

- jogging

- racket sports

- brisk walking

Yoga, which produces relaxation, is one form of exercise that is particularly good for the memory. Headstands and a position called "the candle" are particularly good for memory performance. If you don't think you're quite up to standing on your head, or if physical problems prevent you, you can try just lying down on a bed and letting your head hang over the edge. What's important is to have your head lower than the rest of your body, which has been shown to improve memory performance right after the exercise and for hours afterward.

Get Enough Sleep

Research shows that if you want to keep your memory in tip-top shape, you need to get enough good-quality sleep, including enough dreaming sleep (also called Rapid Eye Movement sleep—or REM). Research from the 1960s shows that people who didn't get enough of this type of sleep experienced memory problems when they woke up. This could be because REM sleep stimulates a part of the brain that replays the day's activities as we sleep, impressing the memory traces on the brain.

Having too little sleep is a problem in particular among older people, who tend to wake up a lot during the night and consequently get very little deep sleep. Insomnia deprives these people of the memory

---

Sleep Diary

Keep track of how much sleep you get for the next week. Write down how you feel each day upon awakening. Do you awake refreshed? If so, you're getting enough rest. If you have trouble waking up and feel sluggish all day, try to increase your sleep by fifteen minutes per night.

	Monday	Tuesday	Wednesday	Thursday	Friday	Saturday	Sunday
Hours	_____	_____	_____	_____	_____	_____	_____
Feelings	_____	_____	_____	_____	_____	_____	_____
	_____	_____	_____	_____	_____	_____	_____
	_____	_____	_____	_____	_____	_____	_____

consolidation that takes place during dreaming and also interferes with memory during waking hours.

If you want to be fresh for the next day, with a sharpened memory for details, try to get at least eight hours of sleep, without resorting to sleep-inducing medications. (They can actually make you feel foggier the next morning.)

Diet

If it's true that we are what we eat, it's also true that what we remember is affected by what we eat. Diet has a direct effect on how our brains function and thus on how well we remember. So what makes for nutritious brain food?

Anything that guarantees healthy brain membranes is a good start, and one such essential food is the right kind of fat—unsaturated fat (especially omega-3 fatty acids). Monounsaturated fats are found in vegetable oils (especially extra-virgin olive oil and sesame, palm, corn, sunflower, and soybean oils), walnuts, pork, chicken, beef, turkey, eggs, mackerel, and herring. Omega-3 fatty acids are found mostly in cold-water fish like salmon, herring, tuna, and sardines.

Exactly how the monounsaturated fats prevent mental decline is not known, but scientists suspect that it may have something to do with helping to maintain the structure of the brain cell membrane.

Research has backed up the benefits of this type of fat. Some studies have found that a diet rich in olive oil (such as would be found in a typical Mediterranean diet) appears to help prevent age-related memory loss in healthy older people. Italian researchers have found that senior citizens who consume diets high in monounsaturated fats are less likely to experience age-related thinking and memory decline. The more of these kinds of fats the subjects consumed, the better they were protected against this type of cognitive decline over time.

While other studies have found that higher levels of education protect against memory loss, it appears that eating the right type of fat also can help protect memory, even among those with low educational levels.

Vitamins

Nutritionists have known for some time that severe deficiencies of the B vitamins can lead to memory problems. While many cases of poor

Diet Plan

How's your diet? Keep a daily diary of what you eat for a week. See how many unsaturated fats you consume. Then, gradually, try to add in more of the right kind of memory-boosting foods.

	Monday	Tuesday	Wednesday	Thursday
Breakfast				
Lunch				
Dinner				
Snacks				

	Friday	Saturday	Sunday
Breakfast			
Lunch			
Dinner			
Snacks			

memory are not eased by popping extra vitamins, it is true that nutrition can influence the health of the brain. In particular, if the body's level of B vitamins drops, memory performance can falter. Niacin (vitamin B_3) may be a memory enhancer, according to some research; in one study, subjects improved their memory between 10 and 40 percent simply by taking 140 milligrams of niacin a day.

Vitamin B_{12} is important to memory, but it can't be absorbed by up to 20 percent of people over age sixty and up to 40 percent of folks over age eighty. For this reason, older people should eat cereals fortified with B_{12} or take a multivitamin supplement—this way the vitamin is more easily absorbed by the body. Vitamin B_{12} problems also appear in those vegetarians who don't eat eggs, fish, or dairy products and therefore don't get vitamin B_{12}. Some diseases (such as Crohn's disease), as well as surgical removal of the intestine, may be linked to lower levels of B_{12}.

Scientists at the University of North Carolina discovered that among rat mothers who don't get enough of the B vitamin choline, the development of learning and memory centers in the brains of their developing infants might be permanently affected. Whether this is also true in pregnant humans is not known.

Folic acid (another B vitamin) has been closely linked to dementia in the elderly; among healthy people, low levels of folic acid have been associated with lower scores on memory tests. This vitamin is contained in a wide variety of foods, especially liver and raw vegetables, legumes, nuts, avocados, cereals, and spinach and other leafy greens. Normally a well-balanced diet provides enough folic acid, but low-dose supplements (200 to 500 micrograms) seem safe. However, taking high doses of folic acid requires medical supervision.

About 5 percent of dementia cases are caused by poor nutrition, especially deficiencies of the B vitamins: thiamin (B_1), niacin (B_3), folate (folic acid), and vitamin B_{12}. Of these, folate and B_{12} deficiencies are most common. For this reason, blood tests to assess B-vitamin levels are a standard part of the clinical assessment for Alzheimer's disease. The best sources of B vitamins are kidney beans, chickpeas, lentils, leafy green vegetables, grains, and orange juice. Vitamin B_6 is found in beef, poultry, and seafood.

Taking vitamin C and E supplements may help protect memory as you age by absorbing harmful free radicals. The antioxidant vitamins C and E can ease stress in the brain cells caused by these free radicals, which are released during standard chemical reactions in the body. Research clearly shows that free radicals damage the brain during normal aging, and also in Alzheimer's disease. Therefore, antioxidants—which can neutralize cell-damaging free radicals—could theoretically help improve memory. In fact, vitamin E has been tested primarily in Alzheimer's disease patients and has been shown to slow the progression of the disease by about seven months.

In one study, vitamins C and E were found to be effective as a preventive to memory loss, helping the men in the study perform better on tests of memory, creativity, and mental sharpness. The vitamins did seem to help prevent men from developing two types of dementia, but not the dementia related to Alzheimer's disease.

In addition, studies have found that men who took vitamins for many years showed a much better improvement, which suggests that long-term use of vitamins is needed to boost memory later in life. Vitamin E acts as a blood thinner and should not be combined with blood-thinning medications or substances such as ginkgo biloba. Ask your doctor before taking vitamin E, especially if you're at risk for bleeding problems.

Columbia University researchers found that patients in the early stages of Alzheimer's who took vitamin E for two years were able to fight off more advanced stages of the disease for a longer period than were those who took a placebo. Participants who used vitamin E took significantly longer to worsen than did the placebo group, although they didn't demonstrate an improvement in symptoms. Experts don't recommend vitamin E specifically for the treatment of Alzheimer's disease because there is no direct evidence that it can treat the condition. However, because previous research has demonstrated that vitamin E has other health benefits, there appears to be no reason not to take it in moderation.

Although patients who have thinking problems may not eat well and could therefore have a vitamin deficiency as a *result* of their dementia, several studies have shown that people with both dementia and B_{12} deficiencies recover when given the vitamin by injection. Other studies have shown that people with folate and niacin deficiencies have experienced mental improvement when they received supplemental vitamins. Unfortunately, only about 25 percent of those with dementia due to thiamine deficiency recover completely when given supplements; another 50 percent show partial recovery. Thiamine deficiency is usually seen in alcoholic patients, but it also can be found among depressed people and pregnant women suffering from chronic vomiting.

Match the food with the vitamin source:

Vitamin A	oranges and tomatoes
Vitamin B_1	meat, poultry, fish, eggs, shellfish
Vitamin B_2	organ meats
Vitamin B_{12}	fish liver oil and liver
Vitamin C	milk
Vitamin D	vegetable oils
Vitamin E	wheat germ

Answers:

Vitamin A—fish liver oil and liver

Vitamin B_1—wheat germ

Vitamin B_2—organ meats

Vitamin B_{12}—meat, poultry, fish, eggs, shellfish

Vitamin C—oranges and tomatoes

Vitamin D—milk

Vitamin E—vegetable oils

Memory Aids

There are a number of memory aids that can help older people keep track of daily information and stave off memory problems.

Keep a Diary

If you notice you're having more trouble remembering appointments, make sure each one is entered into a calendar or diary—and be consistent. Keep your diary in the same place and always enter every appointment. Check the diary every day.

Set an Alarm

Still having trouble? Set a wristwatch alarm to go off shortly before you need to leave for your next appointment.

Lists and Notes

Always keep a shopping list on your fridge or on a bulletin board in the kitchen. Make it a habit to add items as they run out. Keep other lists of "to-do" jobs, notes to yourself—anything you need to remember that you think you might forget.

Write notes to yourself and leave them in a prominent place. Some people find the note-taking ability of a computer to be helpful.

Sense It

If you really want to remember, use as many senses as possible—sound, smell, sight, touch, and taste—to impress on yourself what you're trying to remember.

Relax!

It's hard to remember something if you're tense or nervous about it. Take a few deep breaths and relax your muscles as you try to remember. Try not to *force* a memory—let it gently enter your mind.

Take Your Time

As you age, it may take longer to remember something, but you'll find that the details will often pop into your head if you don't push yourself too hard. If you can't remember certain details, just admit that you've forgotten. There's no need to punish yourself for your lack.

If you're worried about forgetting things, keep a diary to track the things you forget, and when. This will probably show you that your moments of forgetfulness aren't nearly as frequent as they seemed. It will pinpoint those areas you tend to forget.

What I forgot

_____

_____

When I forgot it

_____

_____

Final Note

There's one final thing to keep in mind. If you were never very good at mathematics, you shouldn't expect a few memory tricks to turn you into

Albert Einstein. We all have areas of natural strengths and weaknesses. If memory problems are caused by disease, most memory strategies aren't going to help. But if your brain is structurally healthy, the techniques discussed here should provide some improvement in your memory and problem-solving skills.

Still, while there's certainly no need to accept age-related memory problems as irreversible, you should also be easy on yourself. You may need to set priorities, taking into consideration the lower energy level or stamina common in old age. It's just not possible to run, swim, ride bikes, and do brain exercises constantly. You need to set some priorities.

The outlook is far from bleak. By using the techniques in this book, most older people should expect to regain what they feel they have lost. Barring physical disease, there's no reason for any older person to automatically lose control over brain skills and memory.

Is It Memory Loss or Alzheimer's?

The important point to remember is that as you age, you may not learn or remember as well as you did when you were younger—but you will likely learn and remember *nearly as well*.

In many cases an older person's brain may be less effective not because of a structural problem but simply through lack of use. As people get older, a variety of memory problems become quite common. But very often people who experience periods of forgetfulness don't say, "Gee, I'm afraid I have a bad memory!" What many people tend to tell themselves is: "I keep forgetting where I parked my car. I must be getting Alzheimer's disease!"

The fear of Alzheimer's disease underlies many concerns about a faltering memory. Here's an exercise to help you figure out if your memory loss is normal or something more serious:

1. Do you occasionally forget an assignment, a deadline, a colleague's name?

2. Do you ever leave a pot of boiled eggs on the stove to boil dry? Do you ever make a great sauce to go with that filet mignon and then forget to serve it?

3. Do you forget a word sometimes?

4. Have you ever forgotten what day it is?

5. Have you ever left a jacket at home and then nearly frozen to death on your way to work?

6. Have you ever made a mistake while balancing a checkbook?

7. Have you ever forgotten your wallet, your keys, your glasses?

8. Do you ever lose your temper over a fairly small error?

9. Do you find yourself getting crankier as you get older?

10. Have you ever gotten tired of cooking dinner, working on a hobby, doing your job?

Answers

1. Everyday forgetfulness is normal. But unexplainable confusion at home or in the workplace may signal that something's wrong.

2. Leaving a pot on the stove to boil dry, or forgetting to serve a sauce with the beef is normal. People with Alzheimer's disease might prepare a meal and then not only forget to serve it but also forget they *made* the sauce—or the meal.

3. Everyone has trouble finding the right word sometimes. A person with Alzheimer's disease may forget extremely simple words or substitute inappropriate words, making sentences hard to understand.

4. Forgetting the date is normal. Forgetting where you live, where you are, how you got where you are, how to get home—these are all typical of people with Alzheimer's disease.

5. Occasionally forgetting to wear a jacket or bring an umbrella is normal. A person with Alzheimer's, however, may wear a bathing suit to the store or put on several coats at once on a hot day.

6. Addition or subtraction errors in bookkeeping are completely normal. Someone with Alzheimer's may find that even recognizing numbers or performing basic calculation may be impossible.

7. Everyone temporarily misplaces something like wallets or keys or glasses. The difference between this normal lapse of memory and

something serious is that a person with Alzheimer's disease may put an item in an inappropriate place (such as an iron in the freezer or a wristwatch in the sugar bowl) and then not remember how it got there.

8. Having emotions is a part of being human, but people with Alzheimer's tend to experience more rapid mood swings and even violent rages for no apparent reason.

9. Your personality may change a bit as you get older, but a person with Alzheimer's can experience dramatic personality changes. Someone who has always been easygoing may become angry, suspicious, combative, or afraid.

10. We all get tired of housework, business activities, or social obligations sometimes, but most people eventually regain their interest in activities they once enjoyed. The person with Alzheimer's disease may remain uninterested and permanently uninvolved in former interests.

Other Diseases That Affect Memory

There are a number of other diseases besides Alzheimer's that also can affect how well you remember. While all of the common causes are listed below, we'll discuss a few of the more common ones.

Mild Cognitive Impairment

When you think of "memory loss," Alzheimer's is probably what you think of first, but in fact there are at least seventy different types of dementia that can occur with age. One of the most common is called "mild cognitive impairment" (MCI). More serious than simple forgetfulness, this condition does not affect memory as profoundly as does Alzheimer's disease. Some experts believe it's an early form of Alzheimer's.

While people with MCI perform worse on memory tests than healthy people do, they aren't usually confused, disoriented, or unable to perform the activities of daily living that are so common in Alzheimer's disease. Nevertheless, as time goes on, people with MCI do experience a decline in mental and functional abilities more quickly than do normal, healthy aging people, although still less quickly than those diagnosed with Alzheimer's disease.

Diseases and Conditions Causing Memory Loss

Degenerative Diseases
Alzheimer's disease
Lewy body dementia
Lewy body variant of Alzheimer's disease
frontal lobe dementia
frontal-temporal dementia
amyotrophic lateral sclerosis (Lou Gehrig's disease)
Pick's disease
Creutzfeld-Jakob disease
primary progressive aphasia
Parkinson's disease
Huntington's disease

Vascular Diseases
stroke
vascular or multi-infarct dementia
heart disease
Binswanger's disease
subarachnoid hemorrhage
chronic subdural hematoma
vasculitis

Toxic or Metabolic Diseases
alcoholism
vitamin B_{12} deficiency
folate deficiency

Immune Diseases
multiple sclerosis
chronic fatigue syndrome
immunoglobulin deficiencies

Infections
AIDS
meningitis
encephalitis
neurosyphylis

Systemic Diseases
cancer (brain or metastatic tumors)
liver disease
kidney disease
lung disease
diabetes
Wilson's disease

Trauma
head trauma
dementia pugilistica (boxer's syndrome)

Ventricular Disorders
normal-pressure hydrocephalus
obstructive or noncommunicating hydro-cephalus
nonobstructive or communicating hydro-cephalus

Convulsive Disorders
epilepsy
white matter diseases

Compared to people with more normal memory changes associated with aging, people with MCI have a much harder time with short-term memory, remembering significantly less of a paragraph they have read or details of simple photos they have seen. A person with MCI is likely to forget important events repeatedly.

Other memory lapses experienced by folks with MCI might include repeatedly missing appointments, telling the same joke over and over again, or forgetting the names of close colleagues. In other words, a diagnosis of MCI is made when a person's memory impairment begins to interfere with the activities of daily living.

As its name indicates, MCI is a condition of mild impairment, specifically in the area of memory, while dementia is characterized by additional and severe problems in other areas of cognition, such as orientation, language, and attention. While most patients with MCI get worse, not all will deteriorate. Alzheimer's, on the other hand, invariably results in a gradual decline, eventually progressing to severe, debilitating dementia.

A diagnosis of MCI can be made on the basis of five observations:

- memory complaints

- abnormal memory for age

- mild problems with activities of daily living

- normal general cognitive function

- no dementia

Unfortunately, research does suggest that people with MCI may be at a higher risk of developing Alzheimer's disease when they get older. Up to 15 percent of people over age sixty-five with MCI eventually develop Alzheimer's, or about 40 percent after three years. Only 1 percent per year (or 3 percent after three years) of healthy people age sixty-five develop Alzheimer's. On the other hand, some individuals with MCI never do develop Alzheimer's disease.

Diagnosis

MCI can't be diagnosed by one test alone; a doctor must check both physical and neurological assessments in order to uncover the memory problems that may be abnormal for the person's age and educational level.

Normal memory loss generally associated with aging is characterized by misplacing an item, forgetting someone's name, or forgetting to pick something up at the store. Memory loss associated with MCI is more severe and involves continuing problems in delayed recall of information.

Prognosis

Someday scientists hope they will be able to more easily identify those with MCI and find a treatment that will slow the subsequent development of Alzheimer's disease so typical of the condition. Unfortunately, experts are still uncertain about MCI and how it can be expected to progress. Other critics object to the idea of a separate condition called MCI, and instead believe that symptoms now called MCI are simply a very early form of Alzheimer's disease.

Treatment

While there is currently no approved treatment for MCI, the National Institute of Aging is conducting studies at research institutions in the United States and Canada to assess how well large doses of vitamin E or donepezil (Aricept) may slow the progression of MCI.

Vitamin E is believed to counteract damage from molecules called free radicals). Some experts believe that the progressive loss of brain cells that occurs in MCI and Alzheimer's may be related to this damage. In a previous study in 1997, supported by the NIA, vitamin E was shown to slow down functional decline of patients with moderate Alzheimer's by about seven months by preventing the degradation of acetylcholine, a neurotransmitter that is important for attention and memory.

Stroke

Stroke is another major cause of memory loss. A stroke occurs when a blood clot blocks a blood vessel or artery, or when a blood vessel breaks; all of these problems interrupt blood flow to an area of the brain. A stroke kills brain cells in the immediate area, usually within a few minutes to a few hours after the stroke starts.

When brain cells die, they release chemicals that set off a chain reaction endangering nearby brain cells in the surrounding area of brain tissue for which the blood supply is not completely cut off. Without prompt medical treatment this larger area of brain cells will also die.

Given the rapid pace of this chain reaction, the optimum time to intervene is about six hours. After this, reestablishment of blood flow and administration of helpful drugs may potentially cause further damage.

When brain cells die, control of abilities that that area of the brain once controlled are lost—including memory. The specific abilities lost or affected depend on where in the brain the stroke occurs and the extent of brain-cell death. For example, someone who has a small stroke may experience only minor effects, such as weakness of an arm or leg. On the other hand, someone who has a larger stroke may be left paralyzed on one side or with significant memory loss. Some people recover completely from less serious strokes, while other individuals lose their lives to very severe strokes.

About 30 percent of stroke survivors experience loss of memory and other intellectual abilities. While doctors often focus on the physical disability after stroke, the condition also affects the thinking aspects of a person's life. This type of stroke-related memory loss is found more often among older people, smokers, and those with lower levels of education. Among stroke survivors, the strongest risk factors for memory loss are if the person has trouble understanding speech or speaking, if the stroke is associated with a major disability, or if there is a history of earlier strokes. Other characteristics that increase the risk of memory loss are any stroke that affects the left side of the brain, that impairs walking, or that triggers urinary incontinence.

The memory problems common in stroke patients typically cause dramatically shortened attention spans and deficits in short-term memory. Individuals also may lose their ability to make plans, understand meaning, learn new tasks, or perform other complex mental activities.

Stroke patients who develop **apraxia** lose their ability to plan the steps involved in a complex task and to carry out the steps in the proper sequence. They may also have problems following a set of instructions. Apraxia appears to be caused by a disruption of the subtle connections that exist between thought and action.

Treatments

While there are no proven treatments to reverse memory loss related to stroke, some personality or psychological problems associated with memory loss (such as depression) may be treated or improved through counseling and social support. Worsening of the memory loss may be stopped by preventing a second stroke. Doctors should routinely check the patient's mental status, as well as other emotional and social abilities.

Prevention

The best way to prevent loss of memory associated with a stroke is to prevent stroke itself. You can do this by not smoking, controlling high blood pressure, and maintaining a healthful lifestyle.

Parkinson's Disease

While many people may not realize it, up to 40 percent of patients with Parkinson's disease will go on to develop memory loss and dementia as the disease progresses.

Parkinson's is caused by nerve cell death in a specific part of the brain that leads to muscle tremors, stiffness, and weakness, along with memory and thinking problems. Scientists have found that Parkinson's patients with memory problems also have a smaller part of the brain called the hippocampus, which may be related to verbal and visual memory difficulties.

More than half of all people with Parkinson's disease have mild intellectual changes, and up to 20 percent have more serious cognitive impairments. Typically, however, the memory problems with these patients are not as severe as among those people with Alzheimer's disease. Instead, patients may have trouble concentrating, learning new information, and recalling names.

Diagnosis

Although there is no specific test for Parkinson's, there are several ways to diagnose the condition. Most doctors rely on a neurological exam; brain scans may rule out other diseases whose symptoms resemble those of Parkinson's.

Treatment

There is no cure for Parkinson's disease, although medication and surgery may help in some cases. The most common drug (L-dopa) works well in treating movement problems but is not as effective in easing thinking and memory difficulties. A range of other drugs is often used to control symptoms, but these medications can cause side effects including confusion and even hallucinations.

Huntington's Disease

This condition is a devastating degenerative inherited brain disorder that slowly interferes with a person's ability to remember, walk, talk, think, and reason. The disease usually begins in midlife, between ages thirty and forty-five. Named for Dr. George Huntington, who first diagnosed it in 1872, the condition is now recognized as one of the more common genetic disorders. More than a quarter million Americans have Huntington's disease or are at risk of inheriting it from an affected parent.

Huntington's is caused by a faulty gene on chromosome 4 that somehow triggers a breakdown of cells in certain parts of the brain, leading to memory loss, dementia, and emotional problems. Huntington's is a disorder with an autosomal pattern of inheritance, which means that each child of an affected parent has a fifty-fifty chance of inheriting the faulty gene. Anyone who does inherit the gene will develop the disease eventually.

Symptoms

Early symptoms begin with mood swings and behavioral problems, eventually affecting a person's judgment, memory, and other thought processes. Concentrating on intellectual tasks gets harder and harder, and eventually short-term memory diminishes. Ultimately, patients become unable to care for themselves. The illness may last anywhere from ten to thirty years.

Diagnosis

Genetic testing can accurately determine whether a person carries the gene, but it can't predict when the symptoms will begin. An intensive medical history will rule out other conditions, and a brain scan may reveal the telltale shrinkage of some parts of the brain.

Treatment

Although there is no treatment to stop the progression of the disease, the psychiatric symptoms can be controlled with drugs. Speech therapy may help improve speech and swallowing problems.

Lewy Body Dementia

This common condition is known as "dementia with Lewy bodies" and describes several disorders involving memory loss. The name comes from the presence of "Lewy bodies" (abnormal bits of protein inside deteriorating nerve cells). When Lewy bodies disperse throughout the brain, they trigger symptoms very much like Alzheimer's disease, such as progressive loss of memory, language, calculation and reasoning abilities, as well as other higher-thinking functions.

The disease progresses in different ways from Alzheimer's, however, and includes hallucinations and fluctuations in thinking ability. Lewy body dementia was first described in 1861 and has been more commonly diagnosed in the past decade. It may occur alone or simultaneously with Alzheimer's or Parkinson's disease.

The disease is caused by degeneration in several key areas of the brain, beginning with an area in the brain stem called the substantia nigra. This area normally contains nerve cells responsible for making the neurotransmitter dopamine. In Lewy body dementia, these cells die, while the remaining nerve cells contain the abnormal structures known as Lewy bodies, the hallmark of the disease. The brain also shrinks in certain areas.

Doctors aren't sure what triggers this form of memory loss, although there appears to be a hereditary link. Genetic studies are beginning to find a group of different genes that may contribute to the disease. In certain genetic cases families inherit the condition as an autosomal dominant fashion, which means that if a person carries the gene, he or she will eventually develop the disease. The children of such a person have a 50 percent chance of inheriting the disease.

Symptoms

People with Lewy body dementia have problems with short-term memory. They may have trouble finding the right word, sustaining a line of thought, and locating objects in space. They also may experience anxiety or depression, or acute episodes of confusion that may vary from one hour to the next. Because the confusion isn't present all the time, it may appear as if the person is pretending to be confused.

Hallucinations are also quite common and may occur at any time, although they are often worse at times of severe confusion. The most common hallucinations are visual and involve people, colored patterns, or shapes. These hallucinations aren't necessarily upsetting, and some people seem to enjoy the sensations. At other times some people experience visual hallucinations along with unpleasant persecution delusions.

Some patients eventually develop features more typical of Parkinson's disease, including rigidity, tremor, stooped posture, and shuffling movements, followed later by fluctuating mental performance, memory loss, and progressive dementia. Others experience the memory problems first and then develop Parkinson's symptoms.

The important feature that helps to distinguish Lewy body dementia from Alzheimer's disease is the presence of fluctuations in cognitive performance. For example, one day a person may be able to hold an animated conversation and the next day may be completely mute. It isn't clear why these fluctuations occur.

Diagnosis

There are no specific tests for the disease, although brain scans can show generalized brain shrinkage.

Treatment

There is no cure for Lewy body dementia, although it's possible to treat some of the symptoms. The depression usually responds to antidepressants, and unpleasant hallucinations may respond to medication as well. However, the disease is relentless and progressive in almost all patients, and eventually patients become profoundly demented, usually dying within seven years.

Creutzfeldt-Jakob Disease

This fatal brain disease strikes about 250 Americans each year, causing memory impairment, behavior change, and ultimately dementia. The three varieties of this brain-wasting disease (sporadic, acquired, and hereditary) are caused by a prion—a misshapen protein that alters the shape of other proteins, causing cavities in the brain.

Acquired CJD includes variant CJD (vCJD), linked directly to eating meat from cattle infected with bovine spongiform encephalopathy (mad cow disease). At least eighty people in Europe have died of vCJD since the mid-1990s. Mad cow disease destroys the brain, causing infected animals to act in bizarre ways. It was first diagnosed in Britain, where about 177,000 cattle were infected. Cases also have been reported in France, Italy, Germany, and Spain. It is estimated that about a million pounds of contaminated cattle may have entered the human food chain, and experts speculate that this could result in up to 136,000 cases of vCJD in humans. Because of its long incubation period, it may be years before the toll of vCJD can be determined. VCJD is actually much rarer than classic CJD, and there have been no identified cases of vCJD in the United States.

Sporadic CJD accounts for at least 85 percent of all CJD, and it occurs in the United States but is not linked to eating meat. This form of the disease is found in patients who have no known risk for the disease, which seems to appear out of nowhere.

Hereditary CJD occurs in people with a family history for the condition and who test positive for the genetic mutation in their prions. This version of the condition accounts for between 10 and 15 percent of all cases.

Symptoms

All three forms of the disease are considered infectious but not contagious, which means that you can't get the condition by casual contact such as hugging or kissing, or by sexual intercourse. The first symptoms involve a sudden, progressive memory loss, with insomnia, personality changes, bizarre behavior, visual distortions, hallucinations, and thinking problems. Patients soon lose the ability to communicate and lapse into a coma.

Diagnosis

Doctors use a series of tests (including finding a very specific pattern on brain scans) to diagnose the condition, which can't be absolutely confirmed until autopsy. There is no treatment beyond controlling symptoms.

Circulatory Disorders

Heart problems, high blood pressure, and stroke all can restrict the oxygen available to brain cells by reducing blood flow. Even people who feel fine may have a buildup of plaque in their arteries (a condition known as atherosclerosis), which can eventually limit the oxygen supply to the brain, causing loss of memory and thinking problems.

In fact, researchers recently discovered in one study that men with high blood pressure in middle age are much more likely to have trouble thinking and remembering things when they get older. Men with high systolic blood pressure (the higher of the two numbers in a blood-pressure reading) during midlife were almost two and a half times more likely to have trouble remembering and thinking in old age than were men with low systolic blood pressure. In fact, the higher the blood pressure in midlife, the greater the likelihood of thinking and remembering problems in old age. In fact, for every ten-point increase in systolic blood pressure, there was a 9 percent increase in the risk of poor memory function later in life.

The reason could be related to the chronic damage caused by high blood pressure. Brain scans performed on the patients suggested that many of them suffered tiny silent strokes that caused no symptoms but that permanently impaired thinking. High blood pressure may also damage the brain in some ways that aren't clear to doctors.

Allergies

Allergies are known to slow down thinking and create problems with memory, attention span, and thinking. Many patients with allergies often complain of general and mental fatigue, decreased motivation, moodiness and irritability, slowed or "foggy" thinking, problems with memory, and trouble paying attention, particularly during the allergy season.

Metabolic and Neurological Disorders

Thyroid dysfunction and anemia also may contribute to loss of memory or thinking problems. These problems may go undetected in older people when symptoms are attributed to the aging process. Multiple sclerosis and normal-pressure hydrocephalus (fluid in the brain) are also examples of two neurological conditions that adversely affect mental function.

How to Get Help

If you're really worried about lapses in memory, you may want to consult a psychologist for a memory test to find out if you do have a problem. A psychologist can give you a series of tests of memory, problem solving, counting, and language. Odds are you'll be completely reassured after the tests to discover that your memory is just about the same as that of everyone else in your age bracket.

If your results suggest that there may be some more serious memory loss, your psychologist will probably recommend that you make an appointment with your regular family doctor, who will want to rule out physical causes of memory problems: alcoholism, drug use, sleep disorders, head injury, or any vascular problems such as stroke or hardening of the arteries. Your doctor also might want to check for untreated diabetes or HIV, the virus that causes AIDS. Be prepared to tell your doctor full details about all medications, herbs, or supplements you may take, since these can cause memory loss, too.

Your doctor may order blood and urine tests or a brain scan to help rule out brain disorders. A scan also may show signs of normal age-related changes in the brain. It may be necessary to have another scan at a later date to see if there have been further changes.

If you don't have a family doctor and you're a senior citizen, you may want to consult a doctor who specializes in treating dementia or the elderly in general, such as an internist specializing in geriatrics, a neurologist, a geriatric psychiatrist, or a gerontological nurse practitioner.

If you suspect that you or a loved one may have Alzheimer's disease, you can contact the Alzheimer's Disease and Related Disorders Association (ADRDA) in your area. The ADRDA will be able to give you the names of experts interested and experienced in treating the elderly. They also have information about hospitals that have set up special clinics to treat people with memory-loss problems. You can reach the Alzheimer's Disease Education and Referral Center on the Internet at www.alzheimers.org/banners/5.html, or call (800) 438-4380.

What to Ask the Doctor

If your doctor does find evidence of a dementing disease such as Alzheimer's, you will be referred for appropriate care. If you or someone you love is diagnosed, be sure to ask the doctor:

• What does the diagnosis mean?

• Are additional tests needed to confirm the diagnosis?

- What changes in behavior or mental capacity can be expected?
- What care will be needed?
- What treatments are available?
- What else can be done to alleviate symptoms?
- Are there clinical research trials available?

Drug Treatments

In addition to lifestyle changes and memory strategies, aging people with memory problems may want to investigate certain drug treatments, depending on how serious the problem may be and what's causing it.

Estrogen Replacement

Estrogen-replacement therapy (ERT) after menopause may help slow normal age-related decline in memory, according to a new long-term study from the National Institute on Aging (NIA). By looking at estrogen use in 288 women, researchers were able to examine the relationship between estrogen therapy and short-term visual memory. The study, which was the first to document the effects of estrogen on age-related changes in memory over a long period of time, showed that women who took estrogen performed better on memory tests than did women who had never received treatment. Furthermore, some participants who began ERT between their regular visits to the NIA were able to maintain stable memory performance, whereas women who never had ERT showed predicted age-associated decreases in memory over a six-year period.

Alzheimer's Drugs

As of this writing, there have been four drugs approved for the treatment of the symptoms of Alzheimer's disease; none of them will reverse the condition, but they may put off worsening of symptoms for some months. At least seventeen other drugs are currently under investigation for the treatment of Alzheimer's.

Nerve cells in the brain responsible for memory and thinking communicate using acetylcholine. Research has shown that the deterioration of cells that produce acetylcholine in the brains of people with Alzheimer's disease may lead to problems with memory and thought.

The four approved drugs include: tacrine (Cognex), available by prescription since 1993; donepezil (Aricept), available since 1996; rivastigmine (Exelon), approved in 2000; and galantamine (Reminyl), approved in 2001. All the drugs mentioned here work by increasing the brain's supply of acetylcholine. (Galantamine also affects some of the brain's receptors that respond to acetylcholine.) By slowing down the metabolic breakdown of acetylcholine, they make more of the brain chemical available for communication between cells.

Although these drugs do not affect the underlying disease process, they may temporarily stabilize or delay worsening of memory problems. While some patients do show slight memory improvements, many patients do not respond to these drugs at all. These drugs are most effective if they are prescribed early in the disease, when there are more functioning brain cells available to produce acetylcholine. After too many cells die, the drug no longer works.

As a result, these drugs are approved only for the treatment of mild to moderate Alzheimer's, since they may not be as useful for people in more advanced stages. Currently there is no known way to predict whether a patient will benefit from any of them. Because of this uncertainty, doctors and patients' families must weigh the potential benefits, risks, and costs associated with their use.

Tacrine (Cognex) has been shown to increase cognition in about a third of patients with mild to moderate Alzheimer's disease; unfortunately, the drug does not stop the degeneration of brain tissue, and so it cannot cure the disease.

The Food and Drug Administration (FDA) approved tacrine largely because a thirty-week study showed that high doses improve cognition in people with mild to moderate disease. But since its approval, clinical experience has been disappointing. Depending on the study, tacrine helps only 20 to 40 percent of those who take it. Doctors can't predict who will respond to tacrine, to what extent, and for how long.

Although tacrine can harm liver function during treatment, the risk of permanent damage from long-term treatment is not known. For this reason, patients should have their blood tested every other week for at least sixteen weeks when first taking tacrine to ensure the liver's health.

Liver toxicity affects about half of all patients who take the medication; tacrine substantially increases levels of a liver enzyme to three to five times normal levels about six weeks into treatment. The long-term effects of this rise remain unclear. Other common side effects include nausea and vomiting, stomach pain or cramps, indigestion, muscle aches or pains, headache, dizziness, loss of appetite, and diarrhea. Six out of ten people are unable to reach the maximum dosage due to these side effects.

Rivastigmine (Exelon) works by blocking enzymes that break down acetylcholine. Patients who take this drug show greater improvement in thinking and remembering, in the ability to carry on activities of daily living, and in overall functioning.

The drug, which helped slightly more than half the people in studies who took it, causes side effects including nausea, vomiting, loss of appetite, fatigue, and weight loss. In most cases these side effects are temporary and decline with continuing treatment.

Donepezil (Aricept) has helped some patients by improving thinking, general function, and behavior. Because animal tests suggest that it might also make a difference in less serious memory disorders, the National Institute on Aging is studying the feasibility of using donepezil for people with mild cognitive impairment. Although this drug helps slow the progression of Alzheimer's in some patients, it doesn't work for everyone, and it doesn't cure the disease in anyone.

Many patients can tolerate donepezil, but it may cause diarrhea and vomiting, nausea, insomnia, fatigue, and anorexia. These side effects are mild in most cases and usually last from one to three weeks, declining with continued use of the drug.

Galantamine (Reminyl) is derived from daffodil bulbs and can improve daily functioning and the ability to think for those people with mild to moderate Alzheimer's disease. However, not all patients will respond to galantamine, and no patient will be cured by the drug.

Experts believe that galantamine boosts the levels of acetylcholine by interfering with an enzyme that breaks it down and by stimulating the brain to release more.

In studies ranging from twelve to twenty-six weeks long, results showed that more patients taking this drug showed significant improvement in cognitive performance than did those receiving a placebo.

Galantamine has been approved in twenty-one other countries besides the United States, including most of Europe. The most common side effects are nausea, vomiting, appetite loss, diarrhea, and weight loss.

Summary

While some forgetfulness is common with age, significant memory loss is not an inevitable part of aging. As you age, the connections between your brain cells begin to falter, which affects how easily you can retrieve memories. You can reinforce and add connections by exercising your brain with puzzles and other mental challenges, by learning new information, and by living in an enriched, exciting environment. Reinforcing connections will help improve overall thinking and memory.

As you get older, you may:

- have a shorter attention span
- think more slowly
- need a longer time to learn

You'll probably maintain:

- short-term memory
- searching techniques
- retention of well-known information

Physical changes in the brain that may lead to a poor memory with age include:

- a drop in the production of acetylcholine, a neurotransmitter vital to learning and memory
- a loss of nerve cells in the hippocampus, a part of the brain important in memory
- shrinkage of the brain itself, which becomes less efficient as you age

Lifestyle problems in old age that may contribute to memory problems include:

- unhealthy genes

- exposure to poison

- substance abuse

- poor sleep patterns

- poor diet

- lack of exercise

There are differences between the memory loss of normal aging and the symptoms of Alzheimer's disease. Typical memory loss includes occasionally forgetting words, misplacing things or forgetting where you parked the car, forgetting to serve certain foods, forgetting to bring an umbrella or a jacket, and occasional mood changes. More serious memory problems that may signal Alzheimer's disease include abrupt and permanent behavioral changes; placing items in inappropriate places without understanding you've done so; wearing inappropriate clothing in public (such as pajamas); forgetting how to cook, where you live, or that you have a car. To check out any concerns, you can consult a psychologist trained in assessing memory.

In addition to lifestyle changes and memory strategies, certain drugs may help with severe memory loss linked to menopause or Alzheimer's disease.

SELF-TEST

As a way for you to review what you've read in this chapter, see how many of these questions you can answer without rereading:

1. What is one of the best ways to keep your memory sharp?

2. Why does solving puzzles and riddles help to strengthen the brain and its memory?

3. What part of the brain is especially vulnerable to aging?

4. What are two differences between normal memory loss and Alzheimer's disease?

1. Practice puzzles and challenging games.

2. It builds new connections between cells.

3. the hippocampus

4.

Normal Memory Loss	**Alzheimer's Disease**
forgetting words	substituting words or using unintelligible words
misplacing items	putting away items inappropriately
forgetting where you parked	forgetting that you have a car
forgetting to bring a jacket	wearing inappropriate clothing
occasional mood changes	severe, permanent mood changes

Final Exam

1. What are some of the best ways to keep memory sharp as you age?

2. What part of the brain is especially vulnerable to aging?

3. Why do puzzles and riddles help to strengthen the brain?

4. What is the first stage of creating a memory?

5. To properly encode a memory, what must you do?

6. What are the three ways a memory is stored?

7. If you forget something, the problem may be in one of three components of your memory system. What are these?

8. What can you do to your environment to help improve your memory?

9. Name three poor lifestyle choices that can interfere with memory.

10. What do the letters in the PQRST method stand for?

11. Name three good things to do when studying for a test to help you remember information.

12. Describe one of the four mnemonic methods used to remember items.

13. Name the different types of peg systems.

14. Name three ways you can practice a foreign language that will help improve your memory.

15. Remembering a face requires _____, whereas remembering a name requires _____.

16. Describe the visual technique for remembering a name and face.

17. Describe the verbal technique for remembering a name and face.

18. Why do people forget a name?

19. Name one memory strategy to help you remember numbers.

20. Describe a system for figuring out any day of the week for any date in the year.

21. Describe the method of loci as it would be used for a speech.

22. Name at least two differences between normal memory loss and Alzheimer's disease.

ANSWERS

1. Practice puzzles and challenging games.

2. the hippocampus

3. They build new connections between cells.

4. The first stage of creating a memory is encoding or retaining.

5. To properly encode a memory, you must first pay attention.

6. Memory is stored in the sensory stage, in short-term memory, and in long-term memory.

7. Registering, retention, and retrieval. You may not have registered the information clearly; you may not have retained what you registered; or you may not be able to retrieve the memory accurately.

8. Add as much color, interest, novelty, and challenge as you can.

9. stress, anxiety, depression, use of certain medications or illegal drugs, drinking alcohol, smoking, and lack of sleep

10. **P**review, **Q**uestion, **R**eview, **S**tate, and **T**est

11. Visualize and make information more memorable as you read, take good notes, space out your study periods, study one subject and go right to bed, don't study two similar subjects back to back, don't cram the night before.

12. method of loci, link method, story system, or peg systems

13. rhyming, phonetic, and alphabet peg systems

14. watching videos or listening to audiocassettes in the language, watching radio or TV shows in the language, reading periodicals or books in the language, speaking with a native, taking classes

15. recognition, recall

16. Associate the name with something meaningful. Note distinctive features of the person's face. Form a visual association between the face and the name. Rehearse the name and then repeat it to yourself later.

17. **Register** the person's name: pay attention! **Repeat** the person's name to yourself. **Use** the person's name out loud as soon as possible.

18. They haven't paid enough attention or rehearsed the name enough to register it, or they were tense, preoccupied, or distracted as they heard the name.

19. relationships, chunking, visualization, secret codes, peg systems

20. Memorize the first Sunday in each of the twelve months in code form. Then you can just add seven to get any successive Sunday and count from there to get the rest of the days of the week for the month.

21. Using the method of loci, you write down a key word for each main thought and place it in one of the rooms of your memory building. To recall the speech, you simply go to each room and retrieve each key word.

22.

Normal Memory Loss	**Alzheimer's Disease**
forgetting words	substituting words or using unintelligible words
misplacing items	putting away items inappropriately
forgetting where you parked	forgetting that you have a car
forgetting to bring a jacket	wearing inappropriate clothing
occasional mood changes	severe, permanent mood changes

Glossary

abstract memory General knowledge. This type of memory is capable of storing a great deal of information about objects and events.

acetylcholine A neurotransmitter that appears to be involved in learning and memory. Acetylcholine is severely diminished in the brains of people with Alzheimer's disease.

acquisition Encoding or recording information—the first step in memory formation. People who have a bad memory may have trouble with acquisition if the information was never properly recorded.

axon The tubelike arm of a nerve cell that normally transmits outgoing signals from one cell body to another. Each nerve cell has one axon.

cerebral cortex The outer layer of the brain, consisting of nerve cells and the pathways that connect them. The cerebral cortex is the part of the brain in which thought processes (including learning, language, and reasoning) take place.

dendrites Branched extensions of the nerve-cell body that receive signals from other nerve cells. Each nerve cell usually has many dendrites.

enzyme A protein produced by living organisms that promotes or otherwise influences chemical reactions.

hippocampus An area buried deep in the forebrain that helps regulate emotion and is important for learning and memory.

long-term memory A multilayer type of memory that lasts indefinitely.

mnemonic Any type of memory system or technique that boosts recall.

nerve cell (neuron) The basic working unit of the nervous system. The nerve cell is typically composed of a cell body containing the nucleus, several short branches (dendrites), and one long arm (the axon) with short branches along its length and at its end.

neurotransmitter A specialized chemical messenger (e.g., acetylcholine, dopamine, norepinephrine, serotonin) that sends a message from one nerve cell to another. Most neurotransmitters play different roles throughout the body, many of which are not yet known.

protein A molecule made up of amino acids arranged in a certain order. Proteins include neurotransmitters, enzymes, and many other substances.

receptor A site on a nerve cell that receives a specific neurotransmitter; the message receiver.

short-term memory Immediate, working memory that will quickly fade away unless processed further.

synapse The tiny gap across which a signal is transmitted from one nerve cell to another, usually by a neurotransmitter.

Appendix 1
Associations Dealing with Memory Problems

Aging

American Association of Retired Persons (AARP)
601 East Street NW
Washington, D.C. 20049
(202) 434-AARP

American Geriatrics Society
770 Lexington Avenue, Suite 300
New York, NY 10021
(212) 308-1414

American Society on Aging
833 Market Street, Suite 512
San Francisco, CA 94103
(415) 882-2910

Asociación Nacional por Personas Mayores (National Association for Hispanic Elderly)
234 E. Colorado Boulevard, #300
Pasadena, CA 91104
(800) 953-8553 (in California only); (213) 487-1922
www.health.gov/nhic/NHICScripts/Entry.cfm?HRCode=HR0853

National Aging Information Center
U.S. Administration on Aging
330 Independence Avenue SW, Room 4656
Washington, D.C. 20201
(202) 619-7501
www.aoa.dhhs.gov/naic

Central source for a wide variety of program and policy-related materials.

National Alliance of Senior Citizens
1700 18th Street NW, Suite 401
Washington, D.C. 20009
(202) 986-0117

National Association of Area Agencies on Aging
927 15th Street NW, Sixth floor
Washington, D.C. 20005
(202) 296-8130
www.n4a.org

National Council of Senior Citizens
1331 F Street NW
Washington, D.C. 20004
(202) 347-8800

National Council on the Aging
409 Third Street SW, Suite 200
Washington, D.C. 20024
(202) 479-1200

National Institute on Aging
Building 31, Room 5C-27
Bethesda, MD 20892
(310) 496-1752

National Institute on Aging Information Center
P.O. Box 8057
Gaithersburg, MD 20898
(800) 222-2225

United Seniors Health Cooperative
1331 H Street NW, #500
Washington, D.C. 20005
(202) 393-6222

Alcoholism

Al-Anon and Ala-Teen
Al-Anon Family Group Headquarters, Inc.
1600 Corporate Landing Parkway
Virginia Beach, VA 23454-5617
(888) 4AL-ANON
www.al-anon.alateen.org
e-mail: WSO@al-anon.org

Offers support groups for the family and friends of alcoholics.

Alcoholics Anonymous
AA World Services, Inc.
P.O. Box 459
New York, NY 10163
(212) 870-3400
www.alcoholics-anonymous.org

Information and links to support groups.

Alzheimer's Disease

ADEAR/Alzheimer's Disease Education and Referral Center
NIH
P.O. Box 8250
Silver Spring, MD 20907-8250
(800) 438-4380; (301) 495-3311; (301) 495-3334
www.alzheimers.org
e-mail: adear@alzheimers.org

Provides information about Alzheimer's disease and related disorders. The ADEAR Center is a service of the National Institute on Aging (NIA), one of the National Institutes of Health under the U.S. Department of Health and Human Services.

Alzheimer's Association
919 N. Michigan Avenue, Suite 1100
Chicago, IL 60611-1676
(312) 335-8700; (800) 272-3900
Fax: (312) 335-1110
www.alz.org
e-mail: info@alz.org

Offers information on publications available from the association, refers callers to local chapters and support groups.

Alzheimer's Disease International
45-46 Lower Marsh
London, United Kingdom
SE1 7RG
44-20-7620-3011
www.alz.co.uk

Alzheimer Europe
www.alzheimer-europe.org

Alzheimer's Family Relief Program
c/o American Health Assistance Foundation
15825 Shady Grove Road, Suite 140
Rockville, MD 20850
www.ahaf.org/afrp/afrp.htm

Alzheimer's Foundation
8177 South Harvard
M/C-114
Tulsa, OK 74137
(918) 481-6031

Alzheimer's Foundation of the South
3401 Medical Park Drive
Building One, Suite 101
P.O. Box 9693
Mobile, AL 36691
(334) 438-9590
www.alzfoundation.com

Alzheimer Society of Canada

www.alzheimer.ca

American Health Assistance Foundation (AHAF)

www.ahaf.org/index.html

A nonprofit charitable organization with over twenty-five years dedicated to funding research on Alzheimer's disease and other health conditions, and educating the public and providing emergency financial assistance to Alzheimer's patients and their caregivers through the Alzheimer's Family Relief Program. The group offers a range of free publications.

American Association for Retired Persons

AARP Foundation

601 E Street NW, Room B4-240

Washington, D.C. 20049

www.aarp.org/endoflife

Offers a state-specific advance directive guide, "Planning for Incapacity: A Self-Help Guide." Order by mail, specifying the state, with a $5 check payable to the AARP Foundation. Information on obtaining and completing advance directives is also available at their Web site.

Eldercare Locator

1112 16th Street NW, Suite 100

Washington, D.C. 20036

(800) 677-1116

This service of the National Association of Area Agencies on Aging provides information about and referrals to respite care and other home and community services offered by state and area agencies on aging.

John Douglas French Alzheimer's Foundation

11620 Wilshire Boulevard, Suite 270

Los Angeles, CA 90025

www.jdfaf.org

National Institute of Neurological Disorders and Stroke
Public Inquiries
Building 31, Room 8A-16
Bethesda, MD 20892
(301) 496-5751

Part of the National Institutes of Health, NINDS conducts and sponsors research on Alzheimer's disease, focusing on the basic biology and genetics of the disease and its clinical management and diagnosis.

Partnership for Caring
(800) 989-9455
www.partnershipforcaring.org
Offers free, state-specific living wills.

Aphasia

National Aphasia Association
156 Fifth Avenue, Suite 707
New York, NY 10010
(800) 922-4622
www.aphasia.org

Provides education, research, rehabilitation, and support services to assist both people with aphasia and their families.

Caregivers

Alzheimer's Family Relief Program
c/o American Health Assistance Foundation
15825 Shady Grove Road, Suite 140
Rockville, MD 20850
www.ahaf.org/afrp/afrp.htm

American Health Assistance Foundation (AHAF)
www.ahaf.org/index.html

A nonprofit charitable organization with over twenty-five years dedicated to funding research on Alzheimer's disease and other health conditions, educating the public, and providing emergency financial assistance to Alzheimer's patients and their caregivers through the Alzheimer's Family Relief Program. The group offers a range of free publications.

Children of Aging Parents
1609 Woodbourne Road, Suite 302A
Levittown, PA 19057
(800) 227-7294
www.caps4caregivers.org

Family Caregiver Alliance
690 Market Street, Suite 600
San Francisco, CA 94104
(415) 434-3388; (800) 445-8106 (in California only)
fax: (415) 434-3508
www.caregiver.org
e-mail: info@caregiver.org

Family Caregiver Alliance supports and assists caregivers of brain-impaired adults through education, research, services, and advocacy.

Interfaith Caregivers Alliance
112 West 9th Street, Suite 600
Kansas City, MO 64105
(816) 931-5442
www.interfaithcaregivers.org

National Association of Professional Geriatric Care Managers
1604 N. Country Club Road
Tucson, AZ 85716-3102
(520) 881-8008
www.caremanager.org

National Family Caregivers Association
9223 Longbranch Parkway
Silver Spring, MD 20901
(301) 949-3638

Stroke

National Institute of Neurological Disorders and Stroke (NINDS)
Public Inquiries
Building 31, Room 8A-16
Bethesda, MD 20892
(301) 496-5751

Part of the National Institutes of Health, NINDS conducts and sponsors research on neurological diseases.

Appendix 2
Helpful Web Sites

General Information

National Institute on Health: Forgetfulness: It's Not Always What You Think

www.nih.gov/nia/health/agepages/forget.htm

A government informational page with a link to the Alzheimer's Disease Education and Referral Center (ADEAR).

Mayo Clinic: Memory Loss: Not Always Permanent

www.mayohealth.org/mayo/common/htm/alzheimers.htm

Informative site that is part of the Mayo Clinic Health Oasis. The Alzheimer's Center link leads to information for caregivers and quizzes to test your knowledge of the disease.

Cognitive Neurology and Alzheimer's Disease Center: Glossary

www.brain.nwu.edu/core/define.htm

Provides definitions for the medical terms you might hear while seeking treatment for memory loss.

Cognitive Neurology and Alzheimer's Disease Center: Information

www.brain.nwu.edu/core/caregive.htm

Provides information for caregivers of those with Alzheimer's disease and other memory disorders.

Institute for Brain Aging

www.alz.uci.edu/CausesofDementia.html

Lists the possible causes of dementia.

Alzheimer's Disease

Agency for Healthcare Research: Early Alzheimer's Disease

www.ahcpr.gov/clinic/alzcons.htm

A patient and family guide to early Alzheimer's disease, published by the Agency for Healthcare Research and Quality.

Alzheimer's Disease Cooperative Study

www.antimony.ucsd.edu

University Memory and Aging Center

www.ohioalzcenter.org/warn.html

Lists the ten warning signs of Alzheimer's disease.

The Cognitive Neurology and Alzheimer's Disease Center

www.brain.nwu.edu/core/dementia.htm

Gives a clear definition of dementia, covering Alzheimer's disease and its ten warning signs.

The Alzheimer's Web

home.mira.net/~dhs/ad3.html

A site for patients and physicians that is devoted to Alzheimer's research. It takes a more academic approach.

Alzheimer Society of Canada

www.alzheimer.ca

Provides information about Alzheimer's disease.

American Health Assistance Foundation: Symptoms

www.ahaf.org/alzdis/about/adsymp.htm

Gives the symptoms of Alzheimer's disease.

American Health Assistance Foundation

www.ahaf.org/alzdis/about/adcare.htm

Gives practical information on creating a safe environment and solving day-to-day problems for caregivers of those with Alzheimer's disease.

National Institute of Aging (NIA): Alzheimer's Disease Centers

www.alzheimers.org/pubs/adcdir.html

Gives a list of national Alzheimer's disease centers.

Alzheimer's Research Forum

www.alzforum.org

Provides information and links related to Alzheimer's disease.

Dementia with Lewy Bodies

National Institutes of Health

www.ninds.nih.gov/health_and_medical/disorders/
dementiawithlewybodies_doc.htm

Defines dementia with Lewy bodies, a dementia with elements of both Alzheimer's and Parkinson's diseases.

Lewy-Net

www.ccc.nottingham.ac.uk/~mpzjlowe/lewy/lewyhome.html

Provides information about dementia with Lewy bodies.

Depression

National Institute of Mental Health

www.nimh.nih.gov/publicat/depressionmenu.cfm

Gives information on depression.

Lewy Body Dementia

See Dementia with Lewy Bodies

Memory Quizzes and Memory-Improvement Information

New York Memory and Healthy Aging Services

www.nymemory.org/devig/memoryquiz.html

Gives a memory quiz; provides aging information.

Cognitive Neurology and Alzheimer's Disease Center of Northwestern University

www.brain.nwu.edu/core/memory.htm

Gives a memory test; provides information on Alzheimer's.

Menopause

New York Memory and Healthy Aging Services

www.nymemory.org/devig/index.html

A site for women addressing memory loss in menopause, the effect of estrogen therapy, and Alzheimer's disease.

Stroke/Multi-Infarct Dementia

National Institute of Neurological Diseases and Stroke

www.ninds.nih.gov/health_and_medical/pubs/stroke_hope_through_research.htm

An exhaustive site on stroke—types, causes, and therapies.

National Institute of Neurological Diseases and Stroke

www.ninds.nih.gov/health_and_medical/disorders/multi-infarctdementia_doc.htm

Provides facts on multi-infarct dementia.

Wernicke-Korsakoff Syndrome (Alcohol-Related Dementia)

Family Caregiver Alliance

www.caregiver.org/factsheets/wks.html

Gives a definition of alcohol–related dementia, plus information on treatment and recommendations for caregivers.

Appendix 3
Read More about It

Alzheimer's Disease

Bellenir, Karen, ed. *Alzheimer's Disease Sourcebook: Basic Consumer Health Information About Alzheimer's Disease, Related Disorders, and Other Dementias.* Detroit: Omnigraphics, Inc., 1999.

Cohen, Elwood. *Alzheimer's Disease: Prevention, Intervention, and Treatment.* New Canaan, Conn.: Keats Publishing, 1999.

Davies, Helen D., and Michael P. Jensen. *Alzheimer's: The Answers You Need.* Forest Knolls, Calif.: Elder Books, 1998.

Gray-Davidson, Frena. *Frequently Asked Questions: Alzheimer's Disease.* Lowell, Mass.: Lowell House, 1999.

Hay, Jennifer. *Alzheimer's & Dementia: Questions You Have . . . Answers You Need.* Allentown, Pa.: Peoples Medical Society, 1996.

Kuhn, Daniel, and David A. Bennett. *Alzheimer's Early Stages: First Steps in Caring and Treatment.* Alameda, Calif.: Hunter House, 1999.

Molloy, William, and Paul Caldwell. *Alzheimer's Disease.* Willowdale, Ontario, Canada: Firefly Books, 1998.

Nelson, James Lindemann, and Hilde Lindemann Nelson. *Alzheimer's: Answers to Hard Questions for Families.* New York: Main Street Books, 1997.

Rogers, Joseph. *Candle and Darkness: Current Research in Alzheimer's Disease.* Chicago: Bonus Books, 1998.

Snyder, Lisa. *Speaking Our Minds: Personal Reflections from Individuals with Alzheimer's.* New York: W. H. Freeman & Co., 1999.

Caregivers' Books

Dowling, James R., and Nancy L. Mace. *Keeping Busy: A Handbook of Activities for Persons with Dementia.* Baltimore: Johns Hopkins University Press, 1995.

Driscoll, Eileen H. *Alzheimer's: A Handbook for the Caretaker.* Boston: Branden Publishing Co., 1994.

Edwards, Allen Jack. *When Memory Fails: Helping the Alzheimer's and Dementia Patient.* Cambridge, Mass.: Perseus Press, 1994.

Gray-Davidson, Frena. *The Alzheimer's Sourcebook for Caregivers: A Practical Guide for Getting Through the Day.* Los Angeles: Lowell House, 1996.

Gruetzner, Howard. *Alzheimer's: A Caregiver's Guide and Sourcebook.* New York: John Wiley & Sons, 1992.

Haisman, Pam. *Alzheimer's Disease: Caregivers Speak Out.* Fort Myers, Fla.: Chippendale House Publishers, 1998.

Hamdy, R. C., et.al., eds. *Alzheimer's Disease: A Handbook for Caregivers.* St. Louis: Mosby, 1997.

Hodgson, Harriet. *Alzheimer's—Finding the Words: A Communication Guide for Those Who Care.* New York: John Wiley & Sons, 1995.

Mace, Nancy L., and Peter V. Rabins. *The 36-Hour Day: A Family Guide to Caring for Persons with Alzheimer Disease, Related Dementing Illnesses, and Memory Loss in Later Life.* Baltimore: Johns Hopkins University Press, 1999.

Sheridan, Carmel B. *Failure-Free Activities for the Alzheimer Patient: A Guidebook for Caregivers.* Forest Knolls, Calif.: Elder Books 1987.

Dementia

Rabins, Peter V., et. al. *Practical Dementia Care.* Oxford: Oxford University Press, 1999.

Depression

Mondimore, Francis Mark. *Depression: The Mood Disease (Johns Hopkins Health Book).* Baltimore: Johns Hopkins University Press, 1995.

Perry, Angela R., ed. *Essential Guide to Depression: American Medical Association.* New York: Pocket Books, 1998.

Memory Improvement

Crook, Thomas H., and Brenda D. Adderly. *The Memory Cure.* New York: Pocket Books, 1999.

Green, Cynthia R. *Total Memory Workout: 8 Steps to Maximum Memory Fitness.* New York: Bantam Doubleday Dell, 1999.

Lorayne, Harry, and Jerry Lucas. *The Memory Book.* New York: Ballantine Books, 1996.

Mark, Vernon H., and Jeffrey P. Mark. *Reversing Memory Loss: Proven Methods for Regaining, Strengthening, and Preserving Your Memory.* Boston: Houghton Mifflin, 2000.

McPherson, Fiona. *The Memory Key.* Franklin Lakes, N.J.: Career Press, 2000.

Turkington, Carol A. *12 Steps to a Better Memory.* New York: Plume, 1996.

Yutsis, Pavel, and Lynda Toth. *Why Can't I Remember?: Reversing Normal Memory Loss.* East Rutherford, N.J.: Avery Publishing Group, 1999.

Menopause

Warga, Claire L. *Menopause and the Mind: The Complete Guide to Coping with Memory Loss, Foggy Thinking, Verbal Confusion, and Other Cognitive Effects of Perimenopause and Menopause.* New York: Simon & Schuster, 1999.

References

Acheson S. K., E. L. Ross, and H. S. Swartzwelder. "Age-independent and dose-response effects of ethanol on spatial memory in rats." *Alcohol* 2001 23(3):167–75.

Adler, Tina. "Implicit memory seems to age well." *APA Monitor* (Feb. 1990): 8.

———. "Psychologists examine aging, cognitive changes." *APA Monitor* (Nov. 1990): 4–5.

Baddeley, A. *Your Memory: A User's Guide.* London: Penguin Books, 1994.

———. "Working memory." *Science* 255 (Jan. 31, 1992): 556–559.

Baine, D. *Memory and Instruction.* Englewood Cliffs, N.J.: Educational Technology Publications, 1986.

Biggs, J. B., and P. J. Moore. *The Process of Learning,* 3rd ed. Sydney, Australia: Prentice-Hall, 1993.

Bower, Bruce. "Gone but not forgotten: Scientists uncover pervasive, unconscious influences on memory." *Science News* 138 (Nov. 17, 1990), 312–315.

———. "Focused attention boosts depressed memory." *Science News* 140 (Sept. 7, 1990): 151.

Brayne, C., and P. Calloway. "Normal aging, impaired cognitive function and senile dementia of the Alzheimer's type: A continuum?" *Lancet* 1988 1(8597): 1265–1267.

Carr, M., and H. Davis. "Gender Differences in Arithmetic Strategy Use: A Function of Skill and Preference." *Contemporary Educational Psychology* 2001 26(3): 330–347.

Cary, M., and R. A. Carlson. "Distributing working memory resources during problem solving." *Journal of Experimental Psychology, Learning, Memory and Cognition* 2001 27(3): 836–848.

Caspari, L., et al. "Working Memory and Aphasia." *Brain and Cognition* 1998 37: 205–223.

Covey, Steven. *The Seven Habits of Highly Effective People.* New York: Simon & Schuster, 1990.

Daneman, M., and B. Hannon. "Using working memory theory to investigate the construct validity of multiple-choice reading comprehension tests such as the SAT." *Journal of Experimental Psychology* 2001 130(2): 208–223.

Duzel, E., et al. "Brain activity evidence for recognition without recollection after early hippocampal damage." *Proceedings of the National Academy of Science USA* 2001 98(14): 8101–8106.

Ernst, M., et al. "Effect of nicotine on brain activation during performance of a working memory task." *Proceeds of the National Academy of Science USA* 2001 98(8): 4728–4733.

Fry, Ron. *Improve Your Memory,* 4th ed. Franklin Lakes, N.J.: Career Press, 2000.

Gruneberg, M. "The Practical Applications of Memory Aids: Knowing How, Knowing When, and Knowing When Not." In *Theoretical Aspects of Memory,* vol. 1, edited by Gruneberg, M. M., and P. E. Morris. London: Routledge, 1992.

Hancock, Jonathan. *Memory Power.* Hauppauge, N.Y.: Barron's Educational Series, 1997.

Helmuth, L. "Neuroscience: Neurons fix memories in the mind's eye." *Science* 2001 293(5527): 27A–28.

Hermann, Douglas. *Super Memory.* Emmaus, Pa.: Rodale Press, 1991.

Higbee, Kenneth. *Your Memory: How It Works & How to Improve It,* 2nd ed. New York: Marlowe & Co., 1996.

Hoff, A. L., et al. "Association of estrogen levels with neuropsychological performance in women with schizophrenia." *American Journal of Psychiatry* 2001 158(7): 1134–1139.

Keenan P. A., et al. "Prefrontal cortex as the site of estrogen's effect on cognition." *Psychoneuroendocrinology* 2001 26(6): 577–590.

Lapp, Danielle. *Maximizing Your Memory Power: The Skills You Need to Succeed in the Business World.* Hauppauge, NY: Barron's, 1998.

———. *Don't Forget! Easy Exercises for a Better Memory.* Reading, Mass.: Addison-Wesley, 1995.

Li, K. Z., et al. "Walking while memorizing: age-related differences in compensatory behavior." *Psychological Science* 2001 12(3): 230–237.

Loftus, Elizabeth. *Memory.* Reading, Mass.: Addison-Wesley, 1980.

Lorayne, Harry, and Jerry Lucas. *The Memory Book: The Classic Guide to Improving Your Memory at Work, at School, at Play.* New York: Ballantine, 1974.

Maddock, R. J., A. S. Garrett, and M. H. Buonocore. "Remembering familiar people: The posterior cingulate cortex and autobiographical memory retrieval." *Neuroscience* 2001 104(3): 667–676.

NIH. "National Institutes of Health Consensus Development Conference Statement: Adjuvant Therapy for Breast Cancer, November 1–3, 2000." *Journal of the National Cancer Institute* 2001 93(13): 979–989.

Nordlie, J., S. Dopkins, and M. Johnson. "Words in a sentence become less accessible when an anaphor is resolved." *Memory and Cognition* 2001 29(2): 355–362.

Sramek, J. J., A. E. Veroff, and N. R. Cutler. "The status of ongoing trials for mild cognitive impairment." *Expert Opinion in Investigational Drugs* 2001 10(4): 741–752.

Steel, S., and E. Funnell. "Learning multiplication facts: a study of children taught by discovery methods in England." *Journal of Experimental Child Psychology* 2001 79(1): 37–55.

Stine-Morrow, E. A., et al. "Patterns of resource allocation are reliable among younger and older readers." *Psychology of Aging* 2001 16(1): 69–84.

Turkington, Carol. *12 Steps to a Better Memory: Fast, Easy-to-Learn Techniques You Can Use to Boost Your Memory Power!* New York: Macmillan, 1996.

Index

Printed in the USA
CPSIA information can be obtained
at www.ICGtesting.com
CBHW082153020224
4013CB00027B/120